OVERVIEW

Overview
  Understanding the Fundamentals
Execution is a complex business and has various driving factors. High performance companies usually have the skills in place to drive successful strategy execution. Also, the creation and communication of a clear strategy that's aligned with organizational vision and goals can effectively drive strategy execution.

A company with the speed and ability to act quickly and make decisions is usually better equipped for execution. Companies must also secure employee engagement and capability and execution-focused leaders to implement strategies. Finally, a company must understand how customer demand and allocation of resources drive strategy execution.

Barriers to execution arise when the company has unclear plans, when employees in the company lack understanding of the strategy, and when the strategy doesn't address employee skills and needs and doesn't provide a way to reward performance.

Company leaders should display behaviors conducive to execution to ensure active involvement. This includes setting clear goals and priorities and being decisive. Leaders must also follow through to ensure everyone is accountable. Leaders should empower people while remaining open-minded.

Middle managers must have an understanding of the strategy to be executed and use it to develop their own capabilities along with those of the workforce. They must clarify the message and set performance-level expectations.

Finally, the workforce must execute strategy by seeking to understand the business. Employees must focus on developing capabilities. And they must understand that they're accountable for their performance.

The third cornerstone in strategy execution is creating and managing a culture of execution.

A strong culture of execution must have definitive agreement at all organizational levels about what is valued, and everyone involved must feel intensely about those values.

Also, such a culture values robust dialog, is strategically relevant, has strong shared norms, and rewards desirable behaviors.

In order to create a strong culture of execution, you can follow four steps. Step one is to provide vision and impetus so employees understand why strategy execution is necessary.

Step two involves providing education to employees and offering time for socialization. Step three is providing clear, positive, two-way communication. And step four is creating a reward system to encourage execution-focused behavior.

Crafting a Business Strategy that Executes

Business strategy involves making decisions about what a company should do and how it should allocate resources. You can execute the strategy once it's in place, but without a good strategy, execution won't happen smoothly. To create a strategy that executes, you first need to define the strategy by fully examining the business, its goals, and its environment.

Defining the strategy involves performing three steps – clarifying the mission, vision, and values; reviewing the current situation; and creating strategy direction statements.

The mission, vision, and values statements form the basis of the company's purpose, actions, and aspirations, and clarify why the company is in business. To review the current situation, you examine external influences, internal influences, and the existing strategy. In the final step, you use the information gathered during the first two steps to set targets for how the organization intends to create value in the future.

Good execution begins with good business strategy. An executable strategy must be planned, integrated, measurable, and supportable.

The second step in creating strategy that executes is to develop the strategy. Developing the strategy involves performing four steps: selecting strategic initiatives based on themes; assigning accountability to initiatives; translating initiatives into strategic targets; and allocating resources to initiatives. This topic covered the first two steps.

To select strategic initiatives based on themes, you need to examine strategic objectives, cluster objectives into themes, create a strategy map, assign performance measures, and list actions and choose initiatives.

Once you've selected strategic initiatives, you need to assign accountability to the initiatives, which means deciding who owns the themes and assigning theme teams to execute the portfolios.

The final two aspects of strategy that can affect execution are translating initiatives into strategic targets and allocating resources to initiatives.

Strategic targets are the short-term operational metrics that are linked directly to your company's long-term needs. Because measurement drives performance improvements, it's important that your strategic

Before setting a target, you must ensure that it's essential for success, that the organizational capability is present to achieve it, and that the necessary workforce motivation is there to accept the challenge.

Strategy can place demands on a company's skills, resources, and capabilities, so you need to direct your company's strategy by managing resource allocation. This is achieved by knowing your people and their capabilities, ensuring that managers evaluate the strategy, and connecting the business units.

Linking Strategy to People and Operations

Creating an exceptional strategy doesn't guarantee that it'll be executed successfully. To ensure your strategy is implemented effectively, it's important that employees understand how their work fits in with the big picture. You also need to translate strategy into tasks, and motivate employees by showing them how these tasks contribute to the strategy.

When communicating your organization's strategy to employees, you must explain why the company has made this decision and communicate the strategy constantly using diverse methods. You need to communicate with those who'll eventually implement the strategy and explain its benefits to them. And you should communicate in ways that encourage employees to help shape the strategy.

As a leader, an effective way of aligning operational processes within your organization is to use a corporate balanced scorecard. This comprises the financial, customer, process, and learning and growth perspectives, which outline your company's strategic objectives and measures.

Cascading the corporate scorecard allows its objectives to be translated into smaller tasks for each business unit. During this process, the high-level scorecard must first be clearly understood. Each business unit should then select an objective, ensuring that its scorecard links back to the corporate scorecard. And you must check that the combined business unit scorecards cover all high-level objectives.

Finally, you need to link employees' personal objectives to strategic objectives. This can be achieved by having the right people in the right place, tying incentives to objectives and measures, and supporting personal objectives with action plans.

Good strategy execution depends on having employees with the right competencies in the right places. Essential competencies involve knowledge or expertise of a particular area, abilities such as interpersonal skills, and personal values such as honesty, creativity, and customer focus.

To ensure your employees have the right competencies, you have to list the most important requirements of the strategic position. You must evaluate existing competencies using an appropriate assessment method, and highlight any resulting competency gaps. You then create a development plan to address any existing gaps and monitor your employees' progress.

Monitoring and Evaluating Initiatives

Strategies are only useful when they're implemented effectively. To ensure that a strategy is effective, execution needs to be monitored on an ongoing basis. There are four methods you can use to monitor strategy execution. These include action plans, strategic dashboards, strategic review meetings, and reviewing employee engagement.

Action plans are informed by strategy maps and include individual work assignments assigned to individual employees. Strategic dashboards contain scorecard information along with detailed reports and data that executives can use to monitor the "health" of the company at a glance. Executives review feedback from strategic dashboards at strategic review meetings and discuss any problems with implementation.

Reviewing employee engagement is a monitoring method that complements other methods. Engaged employees help to implement strategic objectives more effectively than non-engaged employees. Management should measure engagement annually using methods that suit their particular organization.

A good way to analyze how a project or strategy is progressing is to conduct a variance analysis. This involves assessing the differences between the intended objectives and end results.

There are four steps to evaluating a strategy effectively. Executives must first analyze management reports, and once they uncover variances, actions need to be agreed upon. The second step involves assessing priorities. This involves determining which variances to act upon immediately, which variances to monitor, and which ones to ignore.

The third step involves planning corrective actions by making changes to one of the key change categories of vision, strategy map, achievement targets, or the program.

Finally, lessons learned from the evaluation need to be recorded and applied to future strategy planning policy.

Strategy ceases to work for a number of reasons. First, a strategy may be appropriate but may have insufficient resources devoted to it. Second, environment changes can affect the relevance of a strategy as people's attention shifts to other areas. Third, the initial issue or problem may have changed, or, fourth, there may have been too many strategic objectives applied.

When changing strategy to deal with changing circumstances, a new team should be established. The team should follow four steps when altering the strategy. First, it should focus on the mission of the organization and its strategic direction. Second, the team should try to coordinate the systems and execution processes already in place. Third, it should discuss ways to realign the culture of the organization to empower people for strategy execution. And fourth, the revisions and changes should be communicated to all levels of the organization to encourage buy-in and inspire behavior change.

CHAPTER ONE
Understanding the Fundamentals

Drivers to strategy execution

Planning and execution are integrally linked. While planning provides the foundation for strategy and is a time consuming and important task, it doesn't get the job done. The execution of a business strategy – the follow through – is what truly determines success or failure.

Strategy is executed over time by managers in every level of a company as they commit resources, programs, people, and facilities to the business strategy. So business leaders concerned with strategy execution need to know who controls which resources and who has the most influence on strategy execution.

To effectively drive business strategy execution, company leaders need to know the company inside and out and discover who actually makes the key decisions. Leaders may not be aware that they're allocating resources in a way that doesn't align with business strategy execution.

You need to pinpoint and then influence those managers whose decisions drive or inhibit business strategy execution. This way you can ensure your managers are allocating resources in a way that aligns with the organization's strategy.

For example, company leaders at a clothing wholesaler want a new product line promoted internationally. However, some key sales managers insist on focusing on the national market, where they don't have to make new contacts to guarantee sales.

Question

How important do you think strategy execution is to the role of company leaders?

Options:

1. Not at all important
2. Somewhat important
3. Very important

Answer

Option 1: You've indicated that strategy execution is not at all important to the role of company leaders. In fact, while day-to-day execution is primarily the focus of managers, it is one of the most discussed issues among senior executives. Executives are accountable for formulating sound strategy and getting results.

Option 2: You've indicated that strategy execution is somewhat important to the role of company leaders. Actually, business strategy execution is a key concern since it can mean the difference between success and failure of the proposed business strategy and the business itself.

Option 3: You've indicated that strategy execution is very important to the role of senior executives.

The execution of strategy is a main responsibility of company leaders. And strategy execution depends on executives to clearly communicate the organization's priorities, and how everyone involved must act, to achieve the stated objectives.

Business strategy execution is the critical business issue and central to the executive role. While strategy execution is difficult, it shouldn't be viewed as unmanageable.

Rather, business strategy execution should be viewed as the main plan that, if followed, allows the organization to attain its goals.

But what drives strategy execution? As execution is embedded in the fabric of business, numerous factors are at work. Whether a company strives to have a high-performance culture or create and communicate a clear strategy, alignment with organizational goals or speed and ability to make important decisions can help. Employee engagement and capability paired with execution-focused leadership ensures everyone's on the same page. Customer demand also drives strategy execution, and effective allocation of resources is central to success.

Drivers of strategy execution

High performance

Companies that tend to have high performance in revenue growth, profitability, and customer satisfaction often have existing skills that enable strategy execution.

Also, companies that have high performance results are often better at clearly communicating goals, strategy, and focus, which drives strategy execution.

Create and communicate

If a company can attain clarity when communicating business strategy, it'll be better able to execute the strategy.

But companies must be aware of the difference between understanding the value of a clear strategy and delivering clear communication on how strategy must be executed.

Alignment

Ensuring your strategy is aligned with company vision and goals helps to drive execution.

A business strategy that supports the mission of an organization, as well as unit goals, will garner more employee support and will be easier to clarify when communicating execution steps.

Speed and ability

Like clear communication, companies value the ability to make quick decisions and act when an opportunity arises, but it's a difficult practice to master. Companies must be able to adapt to rapid changes in order to be effective at strategy execution.

Engagement and capability

Successful strategy execution requires all employees, at all levels in a company, to be engaged and capable. Employees must feel included, interested, and actively participate in strategy execution. As well, they must have the skills necessary to do what's asked of them.

Execution-focused leadership

Companies can use succession planning to groom leaders with strategy execution skills. This ties in with the idea that high-performing companies effectively drive strategy execution.

Customer demand

The demands of customers are consistently driving business strategy execution, especially as technology is growing and changing at such a fast rate.

Resource allocation

How company resources are allocated is another driver, and sometimes barrier, to business strategy execution.

Question

Which examples illustrate drivers of strategy execution?

Options:

1. A high-performance company detailed a strategy to all employees that focused on company goals

2. Keen leaders took immediate advantage of a last-minute opportunity because they knew employees were inspired

3. Plans to fulfill customer demands can be made due to newly-acquired software and the availability of financial resources

4. Shareholder dividend requests result in a plan to increase sales

5. A strategy is devised due to an increased number of skilled business strategists in the talent pool

Answer

Option 1: This option is correct. Strategy execution can be driven by skills existent in companies that are already high performers, as well as by the creation and communication of strategies aligned to business goals.

Option 2: This option is correct. Companies that have the speed and ability to make quick decisions and take advantage of opportunities, along with execution-focused leaders and employees who are engaged and capable, drive strategy execution.

Option 3: This option is correct. Customer demands and the availability of sufficient resources drive strategy execution.

Option 4: This option is incorrect. Shareholder dividends do not often drive strategy execution.

Option 5: This option is incorrect. Having employees skilled in business strategies is not a driver of strategy execution.

Difficulties in strategy execution

Given that the drivers are so complex, execution of strategy can be a difficult and obstacle-ridden business.

Reflect

Think about your own experience of executing organizational plans. What kinds of barriers to realizing strategy have you encountered?

Write down your response or enter it in a text file in your word-processor application (or in a text editor such as Notepad) and save it to your hard drive for later viewing.

You may have cited unclear plans, lack of employee understanding, and a strategy that doesn't address the skills and needs of employees as barriers to strategy execution.

One of the most important drivers of strategy execution is having a clear, well-communicated strategy. Moving ahead with strategy execution without a clear plan is a common barrier. You can't accomplish strategy execution if your plan doesn't consider the resources available in your company. A lack of resources is a chief barrier to execution. Important too is the consideration of the demands of your customers, the business environment, and the company's financial limitations.

In order to successfully execute a plan, an organization must ensure its strategy is communicated through the entire organization and ensure departmental goals align with organizational goals.

For example, a smartphone manufacturer introduced a strategy to upgrade its products in response to customers' requests. Company leaders failed to liaise properly with the Technology Department, so they weren't fully aware of the company's technological and financial limitations. The Technology Department struggled to keep up with new product software demands and current product support. As a result, the strategy plans were unrealistic and the company was unable to fully execute its product upgrade plan.

Question

Which examples illustrate difficulties in executing strategy?

Options:

1. The customer excellence strategy very obviously needs more financial resources than what's available

2. The IT strategic plan does not identify the technology options that are available 3. The strategy involves creating technologically-advanced software

4. Executives make plans rather than just getting things done

Answer

Option 1: This option is correct. Not grounding plans in the financial realities of the organization can be a barrier to strategy execution. Financial limitations should be outlined during strategy planning.

Option 2: This option is correct. Having an unclear and undefined strategy is one of the key reasons why executing strategy is difficult. Make sure your plans are clear and well communicated.

Option 3: This option is incorrect. Creating technologically-advanced software as a part of a larger business strategy is not a barrier to execution.

Option 4: This option is incorrect. Strategic planning is an essential part of business success and a key element in execution.

Your people must know the plan. If you don't communicate strategy clearly, your employees won't understand how their daily tasks contribute to strategy execution. This is the second barrier to strategy execution.

When this happens, the company can suffer from the "silo" effect. In other words, departments act independently of each other and focus on their own goals, rather than being engaged and capable of implementing change initiatives across the organization.

You must ensure employees have a clear vision of the business strategy, understand their unique role in achieving it, and are actively engaged in executing it.

For example, executives at a call center want the company to be at the top of its market in customer service. To effectively realize this strategic plan, the company must ensure all employees understand their role in achieving it. Customer service representatives play an obvious role, but other employees, such as those in the IT

Department, must also understand how their role helps execute strategy too.

The third barrier to execution arises when the strategy doesn't address employee skills and needs and doesn't provide a way to reward performance. You should align your performance measures and reward system with your business strategy. This will ensure your employees are receiving accurate measures of their performance and remain motivated.

Making sure you have execution-focused leaders is also important. There's often a conflict when making decisions between what's good for the company and what's good for the team during strategy execution. Execution-focused leaders are committed to implementing the strategy. They're also committed to rewarding employees who contribute to executing the strategy and ensuring employees have the resources needed.

For example, a software testing company is implementing a business strategy to keep it competitive. It's integrating existing with emerging technology but the organization isn't providing employees with the technical resources and training needed. The employees are committed to achieving the strategy but can't move forward.

Question

Which examples illustrate difficulties you may face when trying to execute strategy in an organization?

Options:

1. Employees think that strategy is for upper management

2. A company believes that all staff members should get the same rewards, regardless of their level of input

3. The planning team is comprised of employees and managers from many company divisions

4. Upper management controls the business strategy execution plan

Answer

Option 1: This option is correct. You may experience a barrier to strategy execution if employees don't understand their roles in achieving strategy. Clear communication should enable employees to connect their tasks to execution objectives.

Option 2: This option is correct. You may experience a barrier to execution if strategy is not aligned with a suitable reward system and the needs of employees are not addressed.

Option 3: This option is incorrect. Having a diverse planning team is not a barrier to strategy execution. A diverse planning team brings more experience and ideas to the table.

Option 4: This option is incorrect. The amount of control that upper management has over business strategy execution is not a common barrier.

Activity - **Strategy Execution Assessment**

You can print this document or recreate the form in a word processing or spreadsheet application and use it to complete this activity.

There are numerous reasons why strategy execution is so hard to realize. Answer these questions to assess whether the strategy in your organization is taking into consideration all areas that may cause difficulty.

1. Are your strategy execution plans grounded in economic realities?
2. Have you considered the limitations of your organization in relation to strategy execution?
3. Do your employees understand the execution strategy?
4. Do your employees understand their role in executing the strategy?
5. Do your employees' actions relate to the organizational objectives, or are they are only doing what's in the job description?

6. What can you do to change that attitude in employees?
7. Does the change initiative address the skills of employees?
8. Does the change initiative address the needs of employees?

Leadership behavior

There are three cornerstones of effective strategy execution. The first of these is leadership behavior. You need to secure active involvement of company leaders to ensure effective strategy execution.

Leaders need to develop a vision for strategy execution by cultivating a deep understanding of their organization from all angles. This unique perspective puts them in a position to effectively design and execute a strategy. Only leaders can make execution happen through personal involvement and focus. They must set targets and goals, foster organizational focus, and select the right people to implement strategy.

While clearly communicating company direction is central to leadership, setting up the processes, people, and policies to motivate and help employees make execution happen is a key function of leadership. The leader must build both an organizational culture and an organizational capability for executing strategy.

So how do leaders achieve this? They have to develop a number of behavioral competencies such as the ability to set clear goals and priorities, be decisive and take action, and follow through. It's also important that leaders empower people and help them develop. And, perhaps most important, as a leader you should know yourself and embody the competencies you wish to see in your organization.

Behavioral competencies

Set goals and priorities

In order to set clear goals and priorities, leaders should first know the business and understand what needs to be done to realize strategy execution.

Leaders may also foster success by focusing on only a few prioritized goals. Three or four priorities won't tax resources, and most organizations need to focus on only a small number of goals to realize effective execution.

Be decisive and take action

Effective leaders must also be decisive and be able to take action. Often there will be delays in plans. In order to exhibit the competencies, leaders must make decisions and take actions that move the process forward.

The decisions leaders make and the actions they take should all focus on solutions. Also, leaders should insist on realism within the organization. That may reveal shortcomings that people have worked hard to cover up, but good execution demands real and workable information.

Follow through and be accountable

Following through is the only way to ensure everyone is accountable. Sometimes having a few simple goals can mean people don't take the execution strategy seriously.

By devising ways to follow through and check in with those involved, leaders can ensure they keep execution moving forward.

Leaders must lead by example and do what they say they're going to do when they say they're going to do it.

Empower people

Effective leaders are also coaches, someone who can clearly communicate what the goals are and provide feedback on how those goals can be reached. Effective leaders will also step back and empower people to achieve their goals. This approach benefits strategy execution as empowered employees feel they have ownership of the project.

Leaders who seek to empower people can also expand employees' capabilities by sharing lessons learned and wisdom of experience. But effective leaders must be in touch with the day-to-day activities and people in the business to grasp how and where experience can help.

Know yourself and your capabilities

Leadership is something that has to come from the person you really are. For execution to be effective, leaders must have strength of character. Leaders must be able to provide an honest assessment of the organization, people, their own abilities, and work to be done.

Leaders need to know their own values and beliefs and have the emotional fortitude to stand by them. They must know their limits and capabilities, and foster honesty in gaining trust from employees.

For example, a company leader knows his business inside and out. He decides to execute three goals that are essential to organizational success based on the available team and budget.

He meets some delays over budget approval for a project plan, but acts quickly, requesting that delayed team members move to work on another project not affected by the wait.

After assigning responsibilities, he schedules follow-up meetings with every team member to ensure they stay on track.

The leader keeps in close contact with employees so he's familiar with the day-to-day working of the office. He offers feedback to employees he feels could benefit from it, but otherwise he steps back and lets them take control.

He also pays attention to the behaviors of everyone around him in case he notices someone who's either having difficulty or excelling. And he makes sure everyone knows he has an open-door policy.

Question

Steve is the vice president of operations at a pharmaceutical company. Select the learning aid Steve's Leadership Characteristics to review how he conducts his leadership.

How does Steve display behaviors conducive to executing strategy?

Options:

1. Steve focused on three goals for the first six months

2. Steve assigned two team members new tasks after they experienced delays with their current tasks 3. Steve halted the project to keep everyone moving forward in unity

4. Steve insisted all employees remain realistic about how the changes will affect them

5. Steve scheduled weekly meetings to keep everyone accountable

6. Steve shared his experience with team members
7. Steve was open to input from team members

Answer

Option 1: This option is correct. Effective leaders should know their business well enough to set clear goals and priorities. To avoid taxing resources and as a way to keep everyone focused, Steve outlined only a few goals and kept them simple.

Option 2: This option is correct. In order to keep the project moving forward, Steve was decisive and took action. He remained focused on the solution.

Option 3: This option is incorrect. Realizing that it's important for a leader to keep the forward momentum in an execution plan, Steve kept the project moving.

Option 4: This option is incorrect. A leader that insists on realism requires honesty from everyone involved about the status of the organization so as not to meet with barriers during execution. Steve didn't insist on realism but instead gave the message that strategy execution will have the same positive results for everyone.

Option 5: This option is correct. An important characteristic of a leader is the willingness to follow through to ensure everyone does what they're supposed to.

Option 6: This option is correct. Effective leaders should empower people and expand their capabilities by sharing wisdom and experience.

Option 7: This option is correct. A good leader should lead with strength of character. As well, a leader should be open to learning and listening to other points of view.

Learning Aid - **Steve's Leadership Characteristics**

Steve is the vice president of operations at a pharmaceutical company. His key strategic objectives include improving productivity and decreasing raw material costs. Steve's been with the company for ten years and has reviewed how similar plants have met their goals.

Steve decides to set three priorities for the first six months – to create an awareness campaign about strategic goals geared toward all employees, to educate each department on simple changes each employee can make to improve processes, and to test run a less expensive supplier of some of the chemical raw materials.

As the team begins to move forward with executing these initiatives, the new supplier runs into delays which hold up the test run. Steve wants to make sure the project doesn't stall so he moves two team members who are working with the new supplier over to help those working on the awareness campaign.

Steve schedules a weekly meeting to check in with everyone on the team and make sure everything is on track. He wants to make the point that change is a good thing and everyone will find the same positive results after strategy is executed.

He also sets up individual meetings with each team member to go over the goals assigned to them, give them feedback on the decisions they make, and hear feedback on the project from their point of view.

The leadership role

The second cornerstone of strategy execution involves having people in the right roles. Responsibility in any organization is divided among many different levels, such as leaders, middle management, and the workforce. Upper management generally decides the strategic paths to pursue and clarifies them for middle management. Middle management makes the decisions that support or inhibit strategy execution. Then middle management allocates resources, which affects the direction of the workforce.

Leaders usually come from upper management and fulfill a number of leadership roles. They are responsible for holding business units and individuals accountable and making decisions on strategy, message, and corporate culture. Both business leaders and line managers are responsible for maintaining the culture and mindset of the workforce and for identifying and developing employees.

Leaders must hold business units and individuals accountable. To do this, they have to clarify expectations and measure results. This ensures that employees know what's expected of them.

Leaders should also identify and reward top performers and address those who are under performing. If you can implement a high-functioning human resources management system you may find employees begin to encourage each other to excel at their jobs.

Leaders are also responsible for making decisions on strategy, message, and corporate culture.

Responsibilities of leaders
Strategy

Executives are chiefly involved in the formulation of strategy and for communicating the strategy, expectations, goals, and responsibilities. This way, employees at all levels are clear on what they're responsible for and understand the goals that need to be achieved.

Message

In deciding strategy, leaders must also cultivate the brand message that strategy transmits to the public about the organization or its products and services.

Culture

Culture is about how a company does things in order to succeed. Culture is key because it limits or supports strategy. Leaders are the main stewards of a company's culture and support it through their words and deeds. Cultures will differ according to the requirements of strategy. For example, an innovation strategy would trigger a very different culture than an operational excellence strategy.

Leaders at every level are responsible for maintaining the culture and mindset of the workforce that reports to them. A central focus is needed so employees understand how to execute the strategy and become accountable for improving their own performance.

As employee mindset turns to strategy execution, employees begin to embody the culture and fulfill their corporate responsibilities.

Employee mindset should also focus on ensuring customers are satisfied. Try to make customer satisfaction a key priority so that your workforce realizes its job security is based on strategy execution success and remaining competitive in the market.

Leaders are also responsible for identifying and developing employees. This requires a significant time commitment because in addition to their regular responsibilities, leaders must also be aware of what's happening at ground level. They must be in contact with employees and know who's coming up with great ideas, excelling in their jobs, or taking initiative.

How you manage your employees as resources will enable you to choose the right people for strategy execution. So you should try to identify and develop employees who support the message and corporate culture.

A global leader in cleaning and sanitizing products identifies three key strategies focused on customer care, R&D, and global reach. The leaders spend time sculpting the company's brand and message. They're strong on personal accountability and expect the same from their workforce. Leaders spend approximately 10% of their workday developing management's skills and ensuring that the correct personnel are in place.

Question

Business Execution

Jillian is the vice-president of operations at a national bank. Select the National Bank Strategy Execution learning aid to review the leadership role details.

Which of Jillian's behaviors help execute the bank's strategy?

Options:
1. Jillian wants to be sure goals are clear so everyone understands their role
2. Jillian clearly communicates that the company cares and rewards loyalty
3. Jillian takes her time selecting line managers she knows will adapt as well as teach her things
4. Jillian gives some space to a manager who's having a difficult time adjusting
5. Jillian listens to her line manager's strategy execution ideas even though she won't implement them

Answer

Option 1: This option is correct. Leaders must hold business units and individuals accountable for business results by setting clear goals and priorities.

Option 2: This option is correct. Leaders take action and maintain the culture and mindset of the organization by communicating the strategy, message, and culture to employees and the public.

Option 3: This option is correct. Effective leaders need to commit a lot of time to selecting and developing people. Knowing your employees and being open to learning and sharing will make for a more successful strategy execution.

Option 4: This option is incorrect. A leader must be decisive and take action in order to keep the execution plan moving forward. As well, a leader holds individuals accountable for their performance and encourages support for the execution plan.

Option 5: This option is incorrect. Leaders should identify and develop employees for strategy execution. Leaders should also have an open mind to learning and the exchange of ideas and experience.

Middle management responsibilities

Whereas leaders are mainly responsible for defining strategy, middle management is responsible for strategy execution. Line managers must understand both the strategy and the workforce assigned to execute it to ensure the right people are in place. They must also deliver the expected performance levels. This involves understanding the strategy and corporate culture and ensuring that everyone in the workforce understands what's expected of them.

Line managers are also responsible for the workforce culture, capabilities, and performance. This entails understanding capability requirements necessary for execution and monitoring and maintaining the mindset of the workforce.

They must create a high-performance culture that supports strategy execution. Line managers must develop workforce capabilities with strategy execution in mind.

As well, line managers are responsible for retaining talented employees, especially in mission critical positions. This particular responsibility requires a significant time commitment for line managers. And senior leaders are responsible for holding line managers accountable for this responsibility and evaluating their performance.

Remember the cleaning and sanitizing products company? It has three key strategies focused on customer care, R&D, and global reach. Line managers must understand how their resource allocations affect strategy execution. They must also cultivate a culture of innovation and customer service. As well, they must develop employee capabilities and performance measures to guide the workforce through strategy execution.

Question

Think back to the strategy execution at the national bank. Select the National Bank Strategy Execution learning aid to review details on the line managers' responsibilities.

How does line management at the bank meet its strategy execution responsibilities?

Options:

1. Line managers know improving productivity will facilitate the retention of talented employees

2. Line managers create a high-performance culture by highlighting the actions of key employees

3. Line managers allocate resources to retain employee loyalty

4. Line managers work to achieve individual performance levels set by employees

Answer

Option 1: This option is correct. Line managers should understand the strategy and culture in order to best facilitate strategy execution and fulfill their responsibilities.

Option 2: This option is correct. Line managers are responsible for developing work unit culture, capabilities, and performance. Talented employees can help increase performance levels.

Option 3: This option is incorrect. Decisions at all levels can affect strategy execution. Line managers must understand strategy so decisions can be made to further execution, not to retain employee loyalty.

Option 4: This option is incorrect. Line managers are responsible for their own performance but these levels are determined by company leaders.

Most managers while maintaining a workforce have the challenge of delegating tasks in the most effective way to get the job done. In strategy execution, line managers are responsible for clarifying performance expectations for each report.

Managers must get across the message that every member of the workforce is expected to step up and give it their all. And if managers set clear attainable goals, employees will be better able to improve their performance because they'll know what's expected of them, and they'll be motivated to succeed.

While line managers monitor the workforce, they must also be held accountable for their own leadership behavior. Managers should exhibit many of the same behaviors as senior leaders in an effort to focus the workforce and get initiatives delivered.

Also, managers should be continuously raising workforce performance levels and clarifying those levels in each report.

It's important to note that, while line managers don't have the power of senior leaders, they still manage an organization's most valuable resources – its people.

Consider again the cleaning and sanitizing products company that's implementing three key strategies focused on customer care, R&D, and global reach. Line managers embody leadership behavior by detailing expected performance and then holding individuals accountable for reaching those goals. Line managers also move quickly, taking decisive action and retaining the forward momentum of strategy execution. And line managers clearly communicate strategy initiatives to keep individuals focused.

Question

At the national bank, line managers have a number of specific responsibilities in getting strategy delivered. Select the National Bank Strategy Execution learning aid to review details on the line managers' responsibilities.

How does line management meet its responsibilities regarding strategy execution?

Options:

1. Line managers know which talented individuals in the workforce to develop

2. Line managers detail expected performance for each employee

3. Line managers look to company leaders to make decisions

4. Line managers set performance expectation at the beginning of strategy execution planning

Answer

Option 1: This option is correct. Line managers are responsible for their own leadership behavior. They should embody leadership behaviors such as knowing the business, being decisive, and empowering people.

Option 2: This option is correct. Line managers should clarify performance expectations so every member of the workforce is clear on what's expected of them in their role during strategy execution.

Option 3: This option is incorrect. Line managers are responsible for their own behavior and should embody leadership behaviors like being decisive.

Option 4: This option is incorrect. Line managers should clarify performance expectations and follow through with employees to keep everyone focused on strategy execution.

Workforce execution support

The workforce interacts with customers, suppliers, and each other so employees are in the best position to execute the organization's strategy. As the main focus of the workforce, employees must seek to understand the business. Employees need to acknowledge the need for constant improvement and understand that they're accountable for their performance and associated consequences.

Actions that the workforce must take in strategy execution

Seek to understand the business

A workforce that understands the business is better able to recognize what it can do better. This awareness enables employees to secure their own jobs.

Leadership must communicate strategy and performance expectations. But it's employees who must deliver on these expectations. And they must proactively seek the resources and assistance they need to execute the strategy.

Acknowledge the need for improvement

The workforce must acknowledge the need for growth of capabilities. Developing competencies takes a conscious effort; it doesn't just occur by going to work every day.

Leaders should communicate to the employees that it's their responsibility to seek out ways to develop new skills and hone current skills.

Understand that they're accountable for their performance

Employees must understand that they're accountable for their performance. This can strengthen their desire to understand the business and expand on capabilities.

Once employees understand the expected performance levels, they should equally expect feedback from leaders. Feedback is an opportunity for leaders to identify and reward top performers and address unacceptable performance levels.

At the cleaning and sanitizing products company, the employees actively seek out the resources to complete initiatives around customer care, R&D, and global reach. Employees develop skills in competencies required for international business. There's also a culture among the workforce of accountability and product excellence.

In order for strategy execution to be effective, an organization must have people who support the strategy and message. Remember, responsibility is shared among the three levels – leaders, middle management, and the workforce.

So having people in the right roles is important. Upper management decides the strategic paths. Middle management makes the decisions that support execution. And the workforce executes the strategy.

Sometimes when strategic execution doesn't come under one business unit's area, assigning responsibility to the right person can be difficult. If this happens, a senior leader is usually given the responsibility for allocating resources and strategy execution.

Question

Consider again strategy execution at the national bank. Select the National Bank Strategy Execution learning aid to review details on workforce focus.

In what ways are employees focused on execution?

Options:

1. Employees know rewarding loyalty will increase productivity

2. Employees share ideas on how to improve operations

3. Employees look to company leaders for a list of skills to be developed

4. Employees know the business well enough to carry out self-evaluations

Answer

Option 1: This option is correct. Employees must seek to understand the business and the benefits in order for strategy execution to work.

Option 2: This option is correct. Employees must acknowledge that they must improve their capabilities and understand that they're accountable for their performance by sharing ideas and seeking out ways to improve.

Option 3: This option is incorrect. Employees are responsible for developing their capabilities. They may receive suggestions but should seek out ways to improve themselves.

Option 4: This option is incorrect. Setting performance levels and addressing top performers and low performers is the responsibility of the line manger.

Learning Aid - National Bank Strategy Execution Leadership role

Jillian is the vice president of operations at a national bank. The banking sector is fraught with mergers and acquisitions, staff cuts, and uncertainty. As the need for efficiency increases, she's leading a business strategy to improve productivity. Executives at the bank have noticed a cycle of low morale and poor productivity, and want to find a way to turn it around. Jillian needs to make sure the strategy's goals are clear so everyone involved can be held accountable for the role they play in execution.

Jillian meets with the board of directors and the CEO to define the message and culture to be developed. Management would like employees to recognize that the company cares about each employee and rewards loyalty and good performance. The team defines the corporate culture by creating a code of conduct centered on the bank's three most important employee values – dependability, discretion, and professionalism.

Jillian knows the employees she selects to help execute her strategy will be the difference between success and failure, so she spends a significant amount of time selecting those people and deciding how they can be developed over time to best help her execute the strategy. She communicates with line managers the two key goals to be accomplished in the first six months – to revamp the employee benefits program and to create a program that meets the bank's commitment to internal promotion and employee development.

She wants to ensure the line managers are supporting the goals in the decisions they make and how they communicate with the workforce. She runs into a problem with the line manager in the check sorting unit. He's making decisions that benefit him and don't align with strategy.

Jillian takes action to prevent strategy execution from stalling. She discovers the manager is hoping for a promotion and feels since his department has productivity issues, he doesn't need to support the initiatives. Jillian clarifies for him the importance of employees at every level supporting execution and working together toward the common goals. She stresses that she will hold all departments accountable for their part in the execution of the strategy.

She decides to set up weekly meetings with line managers to check in with everyone and stay current. She knows a number of her line managers will be able to take guidance and run with it to really accomplish any goal set out for them.

She also wants to keep an eye on the mindset of the workforce to make sure there isn't a disconnect between executing goals and the message received by the workforce.

Jillian finds her line managers have a lot of great ideas in the weekly meetings and, while they do rely on her as the voice of experience, she's also learned a lot about the workings of the bank that she can apply to strategy execution going forward.

Line managers' responsibilities

The majority of line managers at the bank value the strategy and understand the need for its implementation. They know that improving productivity will benefit them and the workforce – and ensure that the bank prospers in the face of tough competition. They're also in touch with the day-to-day workings of their employees and work to communicate the strategy clearly and focus employees on the two initial goals.

In order to meet performance levels, line managers cultivate a culture of high performance. They clarify expectations of everyone involved in each report so all members of staff understand their role in strategy execution.

They identify and develop specific individuals who have been with the bank a number of years and have high productivity levels in their business unit. Line managers have two goals in developing these particular employees – the employees support strategy execution and will keep it moving forward and it's the line manager's responsibility to retain valuable employees.

Workforce focus

Nonmanagers at the bank respond well to the strategic message that the company cares about each employee and rewards loyalty. At the base level, employees have the benefit of understanding how strategy execution will make their jobs easier. Top performers strive to meet performance levels and spur on fellow employees to do the same. They help spread the message and cultivate a culture of high performance.

Employees share productivity ideas with line managers and this helps the workforce as a whole understand what they can do better to execute strategy.

They also seek more responses from line managers on how they're performing so they're better aware of which of their actions affect productivity negatively.

Learning Aid - Roles and Responsibilities

Responsibility for strategy execution in any organization is divided among many different levels, such as leaders, middle management, and the workforce. Each level has specific roles and responsibilities that must be fulfilled for effective execution of business strategy.

Leaders	Middle management	Workforce
Leaders must hold business units and individuals accountable for results	Line managers must understand the strategy and culture	Employees must seek to understand the business
Leaders decide on strategy, the message, and corporate culture	Line managers are responsible for work unit culture, capabilities, and performance	Employees must acknowledge that they must constantly grow their capabilities and develop new capabilities
Leaders are responsible for the culture and mindset of the workforce that reports to them	Line managers are responsible for their own leadership behavior	Employees must understand that they're accountable for their performance and the consequences
Leaders must commit a lot of time to selecting and developing people who can support strategy execution	Line managers must clarify performance expectations for each report	

Culture of execution

It's no good having all tiers of the organizational chart focused on getting things done if the company culture simply doesn't support delivering on plans. The third cornerstone is creating and managing a culture of execution.

Culture can be defined as the shared beliefs, attitudes, and behaviors of employees in an organization. So when it comes time to execute a strategy, it shouldn't be viewed as a one-time event. Instead, it's an intrinsic element of that organizational culture that is ongoing. So to effectively execute a strategy, you sometimes need to make changes to corporate culture to produce results.

Reflect

Think about how hard it can be to realize plans. What do you think are the benefits of putting in place a culture that promotes execution?

Write down your response or enter it in a text file in your word-processor application (or in a text editor such as Notepad) and save it to your hard drive for later viewing.

Perhaps you thought of benefits such as the increased likelihood that your company will follow through on its promises. Other benefits include having your workforce aligned toward the same goals, having a clear direction, and feeling appreciated.

Strategy execution requires a specific set of behaviors and techniques. In order to produce strategic results, you need to change the corporate culture to focus on those goals. In other words, you need to change people's behavior.

In order to change behaviors, company leaders need to identify relevant beliefs. Then you can work to change the reward system, which is embedded in culture. Throughout these changes you should use robust communication, always link culture to strategy, and use the power of shared norms.

Actions for changing corporate culture

Identify relevant beliefs

Changing the beliefs and behaviors of employees is not an easy task, especially since an organization's culture is often ingrained. If you think about behaviors as beliefs in action, you can create a culture of execution by focusing on identifying and changing beliefs that influence behavior.

For example, a company leader may believe that team building between individual employees is more important than creating a cohesive team.

Change the reward system

The corporate culture defines which employee actions are respected and rewarded. If a company rewards people for strategy execution focused behaviors, the corporate culture will also shift.

Make sure your reward system doesn't simply focus on measurable results like sales figures or new client acquisitions. It must also reward desirable behavior that supports execution. Try to set goals to get people excited, inspired, and motivated to take ownership of the execution plan.

For example, a company's sales associates with the lowest sales performance sit in the front row at a company meeting.

Use robust communication

You must also ensure you have robust dialog and clear communication throughout all levels of the organization when creating a culture of execution.

Everyone involved must be willing to be realistic about the situation and open to discussion. This approach helps create real conversations, ideas, and solutions.

For example, company leaders must be realistic and ensure the organization is free from segregation and favoritism. They must set an example and be willing to exchange ideas with all employees.

Link culture to strategy

It's also important to create a strong culture that is strategically relevant. This is characterized by two qualities: definitive agreement at all organizational levels about what is valued and definitive agreement about the importance of those values.

Sometimes a strong culture fails to materialize because groups agree on company values but disagree on which aspects of that value take priority.

For example, if your company values customer service but departments disagree on the priority of customer needs versus product design, a strong culture will likely be nonexistent. And sometimes it's simply because employees aren't inspired to deliver on strategic objectives.

Use shared norms

You must also take advantage of the power of shared norms within an organization. Different from formal rules, norms can be defined as socially shared standards that lead individuals to conform.

Group norms often have a degree of social control over employees. They sometimes dictate how people perceive each other, how they make decisions, and how problems are solved. So when trying to change behaviors, you can alter shared norms and create strategy execution focused behaviors.

For example, a company with strong shared norms dictated what amount of work was acceptable. This caused normally high-achieving employees to change their behavior to do less work in order to fit in and avoid being alienated. It also caused low achievers to increase performance to avoid similar treatment.

Consider this example. A national public transportation company has a strategy to move a high volume of passengers efficiently and at a low cost. It's able to execute that strategy due to a strong culture. First, company leaders work to change the corporate culture to one so focused on safety it's detrimental to efficiency.

Employees are in agreement that providing efficient and cost effective transportation to the public is of value and a priority. They have a lot to say on the topic and are glad to have a chance to voice their concerns and ideas. The whole company unites around those common values and all employees feel they're a part of something larger than themselves. This excites employees and inspires them to achieve meaningful goals set by the company.

Also, the company changes the reward system to reward those employees whose behavior goes above and beyond what's needed to keep trains running and customers happy. Employees are focused on the strategy and make decisions that help execute it.

Question

Which examples describe cultures that support execution?

Options:

1. Management and telesales staff are encouraged to share ideas on best sales techniques to help execute the sales strategy

2. A company rewards gift certificates to the two employees who receive the most positive customer reviews

3. Employees feel strongly that customer satisfaction is most important

4. Employees agree that safety is a concern but think productivity is more important

5. A company devises a program to reward manufacturing plant employees based on product sales

Answer

Option 1: This option is correct. A strong culture that executes strategy must value robust dialog and have a focus that's strategically relevant. Sharing best practices is connected to increasing sales.

Option 2: This option is correct. In order to promote a strong culture that's focused on strategy execution, a company creates an incentive program to motivate employees.

Option 3: This option is correct. In companies where the culture supports strategy execution, employees agree about what's valued and are intensely committed to those values.

Option 4: This option is incorrect. A culture fails when employees agree about what's important but aren't inspired to take the extra steps to execute strategy, or when they agree on what's valued but don't agree on how those values are prioritized.

Option 5: This option is incorrect. A strong culture agrees on values and rewards accordingly to get employees on board. By rewarding manufacturing plant employees on numbers they have no control over, employees are neither inspired nor motivated to improve.

Provide vision and impetus

Now that you have an idea what makes up a strong culture of execution, you have to determine how to achieve it in your own organization. You can follow four steps to manage and create a culture that supports business execution: provide vision and impetus, offer education and time for socializing, communicate, and reward.

It's vital to strategy execution that employees at all levels understand where the company is trying to go. You must provide a picture of the end result and explain why this cultural change is good for everyone. So for step one, provide vision and impetus, you must have clear reasons for change. As a company leader you must also live the change and set the example. And you must get agreement from key players so everyone is on the same page.

Actions for providing vision and impetus
Have clear reasons for change

You should provide everyone involved with clear and honest reasons for strategy execution. Most business strategies are designed to improve an aspect of the business, so you have to explain how that aspect is progressing.

If you can clearly show employees a record of poor performance and demonstrate how strategy execution will improve it, it'll be easier for them to accept the change and work together.

For example, leaders at a healthcare company demonstrate the need for diversification by showing staff turnover figures for the previous five years.

Live the change

The leader of strategy execution is the person who first communicates vision and impetus. So to set the example for the whole organization, you should also live the change.

Your actions will speak louder than words with regard to strategy execution. And if you embody the values of the new culture of execution, employees will likely follow suit.

For example, in a company with a strategic focus on customer care excellence, the VP of production attends all major customer meetings himself.

Get agreement from key players

A strong culture of execution requires that all key players agree on the vision. Effective strategy execution can only happen if employees at all levels buy in. But before that can happen, employees in all key roles must also be actively involved and in agreement.

For example, the CEO explains the strategy to key executives so they can all weigh in and state their agreement.

Consider this example. The CEO of an electronics company explains to the company that in the past four years, their main competitor has put out 67 new products compared to their 25. She points out that she has held a number of meetings with innovators in the sector and her board. The CEO and her executive team then present the strategy – of maximizing innovation – and its strategic initiatives to the company to great applause.

The CEO is providing vision and impetus for the new strategy. She has solid reasons for change: the company is failing to remain competitive.

The CEO is living the change by engaging with innovators in the sector.

Finally, by having her team present the strategy, she's showing a united front regarding the strategy.

Question

A nationwide chain of department stores is trying to execute a business strategy focused on customer service. Select the Nationwide Department Store Culture of Execution learning aid to review how it created a culture of execution.

Does the CEO effectively provide vision and impetus?

Options:

1. The CEO clearly communicates areas of poor performance provided by customer feedback 2. The CEO lives the change

3. The CEO gets agreement from key players

4. The CEO identifies relevant beliefs

Answer

Option 1: This option is correct. The CEO provides vision and impetus by indicating without a doubt where the store is failing in customer service. This clearly shows everyone why a change is needed.

Option 2: This option is correct. The CEO lives the change, taking an active role and working side by side with staff members to illustrate new values and methods.

Option 3: This option is incorrect. The CEO fails to get agreement from her team. Employees at all levels control strategy execution, so getting consensus from the start is key.

Option 4: This option is incorrect. It's necessary to identify beliefs in order to change corporate culture. However, this is not part of providing impetus and vision.

Education and socializing

The second step when creating and managing a culture of execution is providing employees with adequate education and allowing time for employees to socialize with coworkers.

Providing education

To ensure employees understand the new culture, you must train everyone on the new set of values, beliefs, and behaviors.

This includes any new processes, methods, ways of doing things, values, and beliefs.

It's important that employees experience both traditional classroom learning and hands-on training. This allows them to take what they learn to another level with peer-based discussions. This validates the new culture and solidifies it among employees.

Allowing time to socialize

Ensuring employees have time to socialize will accomplish two goals. First, it'll ensure that employees learn company values, behavior expectations, and social norms. Second, it will encourage bonding among employees, which will help create a strong culture of execution.

Remember, in order for a company to have a strong culture, it must ensure employees agree on company values and on the importance of those values. Socialization helps to facilitate both those elements of creating and managing a culture of execution.

Consider again the electronics company using innovation to regain its market share. Two-day sessions are scheduled to teach employees how to use the new inter-company innovation software and discuss ways of transforming ideas into products. The software enables employees to share ideas, offer feedback, and pass along helpful information. Most of the second day, however, is free time for employees to mingle, try out the new software, and start talking about how they can be involved in strategy execution.

Question

Consider again the nationwide chain of department stores that is trying to execute a business strategy focused on customer service. Select the Nationwide Department Store Culture of Execution learning aid to review how it created a culture of execution.

How are employees educated and given time for socializing during the change to a culture of execution?

Options:

1. Employees are given a chance to share ideas on how to use the new device 2. A new device is introduced to encourage better customer service

3. A classroom-based session is held to teach employees how to use the device 4. Employees at every level are offered training on the new device

Answer

Option 1: This option is correct. After the introduction of the new handheld device, employees are given an opportunity to socialize. This enables them to share ideas, bond, and get excited about the new focus.

Option 2: This option is correct. Employees are offered a new tool to help them with their end goal which also strengthens the focus on the values, beliefs, and behaviors of the new culture of execution.

Option 3: This option is incorrect. The company neglects to hold traditional learning sessions to teach employees how to use the new tool.

Option 4: This option is incorrect. Employees who work on the floor are given the chance to learn the new device, but the opportunity is not extended to others in the company. If it was, there could be more opportunity for shared ideas and bonding between different organizational levels.

Communicate and reward

The third step to create a strong culture of execution is to communicate. Effective communication leads to genuine understanding of strategy execution. And communication gives further credibility to the vision and reasoning behind the strategy. Communication must be clear, effective, and positive, and it must be directed at the people affected. Also, to be truly effective, communication must be two-way.

The attributes of good communication

Clear, effective, and positive

Your communication must be clear, effective, and positive. This is the time to really make an impression on everyone involved by clarifying the need for change.

You should make sure your communication, whether it involves informal conversations or formal documents, maximizes effectiveness. And when you explain how a strong culture is going to execute strategy, you must be positive and upbeat so that your message is infectious.

For example, you could detail strategy execution steps using examples of employee flexibility when serving customers to accentuate the advantages of remaining competitive.

Directed at people affected

All communication must be directed at the people affected by the changes. If you're trying to create a company-wide culture of execution, then you need to address the whole company.

Alternatively, if your strategy affects only a small group of people, you must ensure your communication is directed at and designed especially for them.

Two-way

It's important that you ensure you have two-way communication – bottom up and top down. This means employees being able to pass information along to upper management as easily as upper management sends messages to employees.

Try to break the boundaries of hierarchy in the organization and encourage free-flowing information from employees at all levels. This type of conversation will ensure your culture of execution is taking every advantage to learn, grow, and change together.

For example, a company leader requests that all employees speak freely to one another, regardless of job title or seniority.

The fourth step when changing your corporate culture to one of execution is to reward. You can use a reward system to manage culture of execution by encouraging or discouraging certain behavior. But behavior isn't the only thing to reward. You must also measure and reward performance. Measure performance in connection to whether employees embody the values and behaviors of the culture of execution.

Using of a reward system to manage a culture of execution

Manage culture of execution

If you reward and promote people for strategy execution focused behaviors, the corporate culture will also shift.

The bottom line is that if you link your reward system to the new corporate culture, you can strengthen that culture. If employees are aware that behaviors are connected to rewards, they'll be more likely to begin exhibiting those desired behaviors.

For example, a company that's focused on revenues distributes hand-written thank you notes from managers to employees who exhibit revenue generating behavior.

Measure and reward performance

Business strategy is designed to improve performance but strategy can't be executed without a strong culture of execution. So to create a strong culture of execution, you must measure – and reward – employee performance against the values and behaviors that this culture entails. In other words, behavior that helps execute strategy includes meeting performance goals.

Simply saying you want employees to embody new values and behaviors focused on strategy execution isn't enough. You need to be able to produce measured results in order for a formal reward system to be most effective.

For example, a company measures and rewards top performers who sign on a certain number of new clients while remaining honest and ethical.

Think back again to the electronics company. The CEO takes every advantage to speak to employees, clients, customers, and the general public about company aims. She also encourages employees in all levels of the company to offer ideas. An electronic bulletin board is created so people can post questions, thoughts, or solutions to other employees' problems. And she introduces a company-wide contest for a luxury vacation for the family of the employee with the best product design idea.

The CEO worked hard to spread a clear, effective, and positive message. She spoke with everyone she met, directing the message to all people who were going to be affected by the changes. And she encouraged two-way conversations with employees to get their ideas and feedback.

The CEO also wants to link the values and behaviors of the new culture of execution to the reward system and get employees excited about making changes.

Question

Consider again the nationwide chain of department stores that is trying to execute a business strategy focused on customer service. Select the Nationwide Department Store Culture of Execution learning aid to review how it created a culture of execution.

How does the new culture of execution communicate with and reward employees?

Options:

1. The company rewards culture of execution-focused behaviors

2. The CEO speaks to employees, clients, and customers

3. The company links performance results to the embodiment of new cultural values

4. The CEO encourages two-way communication

Answer

Option 1: This option is correct. The department store manages its culture of execution through a reward system by creating regional and national competitions with great prizes for the group of employees who get top customer feedback.

Option 2: This option is correct. Communication must be clear, effective, and positive, and it must be directed at people affected. The CEO takes every opportunity to speak to everyone affected.

Option 3: This option is incorrect. To ensure performance is measured and then rewarded, the company should award the top prize to the store with the best sales and most positive customer feedback.

Option 4: This option is incorrect. The CEO asks employees to hold back their ideas or concerns, and to trust her when trying the new methods and behaviors expected of them.

Learning aid - Nationwide Department Store Culture of Execution

A nationwide department store chain has been receiving negative customer service feedback. In-store managers and retail employees are primarily focused on getting products to the shelves, rather than speaking to customers and helping them with their retail needs. The CEO comes up with a business strategy focused on improving customer service and being more proactive in anticipating customer needs. She convenes a board meeting on the strategy, and although she does not reach consensus with her management team, she goes ahead with the plan.

The CEO doesn't hold back when talking to employees about how going that extra mile can create customer loyalty. She gives a presentation in each store to give employees some examples of the customer feedback such as "the store is too big to easily find products" and "it's too hard to find help when you need it." She projects the online feedback on a wall of the warehouse. This way, no one can ignore the poor customer service performance.

She goes to individual stores and works shifts with retail staff members while managers stay focused on receiving inventory. She wants to show retail staff members how easy it is to think like a customer if you know almost every product in the store. She interacts with customers, helping them find what they're looking for, anticipating their needs, and taking extra steps to be helpful.

The company introduces a new handheld device for floor employees to use when helping customers. When a query is entered on whether a product is in stock, it automatically displays other products the customer may also be looking for. The company holds a staff appreciation day to kick off the new tool and give floor employees a chance to get familiar with it and learn by doing.

The CEO takes it upon herself to be the voice of change. She is constantly speaking to employees, clients, and customers to spread the message that everyone in the company is committed to delivering excellence in customer service. She is always cautious and mentions that with so many stores it's hard to get everyone on the same page – but that everyone's heart is in it. She also asks employees to let their actions speak for themselves and to trust her judgment when trying out the new way of doing things.

The CEO also wants to connect performance measures to the new focus. She wants employees to let go of the old ideas about getting products on the shelf and embrace the new idea that the customer comes first and the more assistance they get, the more need there'll be for inventory. She decides to create a competition between stores in each region to recognize employees who receive excellent customer feedback. A top performer within a store is awarded an all-inclusive vacation. And to really motivate her employees, the top performer within the region wins a new car.

CHAPTER TWO
Crafting a Business Strategy that Executes

Define the strategy

Without a clear plan of action, most businesses wouldn't be able to operate effectively. Think about it – if managers made decisions without considering their impact, things would fall apart pretty quickly.

That's where strategy comes into play. Business strategy involves making decisions about what the company should do and how it should allocate resources. These decisions should take into account current competitive conditions and growth opportunities in the industry. Remember, good execution begins with good strategy.

The first stage in strategy formulation is to define the strategy. To develop a truly focused strategy, you must fully examine the business, its goals, and its environment. An effective and focused strategy is essential because it helps your company build a favorable competitive position.

The process of defining the strategy has three steps:

- clarify the company's mission, vision, and values
- review the current situation with an emphasis on internal and external influences and the existing strategy, and
- create strategy direction statements.

Clarify the mission, vision, and values

The first step in defining the strategy is to clarify the mission, vision, and values. These three items form the basis of the company's purpose, actions, and aspirations. Essentially, they clarify why the company is in business. The executive team should return regularly to the mission, vision, and values statements, as they tend to remain stable over time.

Mission

The mission statement is typically a one- or two-sentence statement that explains your company's purpose. It should also describe what your company provides to customers or clients. Finally, it should define the overall goal that employees and executives are pursuing.

An example of a mission statement is, "Our company is dedicated to providing the highest quality innovative products so customers always trust our brand."

Vision

The vision statement outlines the company's mid- to long-term goals. This generally encompasses a three- to ten-year period. This statement is focused on the market and describes how the company wants to be perceived by the world. The vision statement usually contains ambitious goals and a time frame for achieving them, as well as a clear measure of success.

An example of a vision statement is, "Our company aims to become the top-selling company in our industry by the end of the year."

Values

The values statement reflects the company's core values. These are the ways the company defines its attitudes, character, and behavior.

An example of a values statement is, "We believe that companies should do their part to protect the environment. Our company considers the environmental impact of all decisions."

Before they can define strategy, leaders and managers need to agree on the mission, values, and vision statements. The mission and values statements don't tend to vary from year to year. The vision statement isn't as stable but typically remains constant during a company's three- to five-year strategic plan.

Consider this example. Jarod is a top manager at an international educational book retailer. He and the rest of the management team are meeting to define their company's strategy for the next year. The first thing they do is develop the mission, vision, and values statements.

Example - See each type of statement to find out what Jarod and his team come up with.

Mission

"Our mission is to provide top-quality educational products, a diverse selection of books, and a wide variety of general merchandise to an international audience. Our goal is to be the most knowledgeable, helpful booksellers in the sector."

Vision

"Our vision is to become one of the world's top sellers of educational books with five million online customers by the end of five years."

Values

"We believe that educational books are the key to advancing society. Customer satisfaction is our ultimate goal and we strive to ensure that we meet the needs of each and every customer."

Question

A company that provides online scientific educational materials is writing its mission, vision, and values statements. Match each type of statement to its appropriate example.

Options:

A. Mission
B. Vision
C. Values

Targets:

1. "Our company aims to provide online scientific and educational material and support to science educators at all levels. We hope to foster learning and academic excellence by working with scientists and educators to create an environment conducive to breakthrough science."

2. "We want to be the world leader in scientific educational products that enable and transform the way science educators communicate scientific information."

3. "Our company is committed to the highest standards of ethics and integrity. We are responsible to our customers, our employees, and their families."

Answer

1. This is an example of a company's mission statement. The mission statement explains a company's purpose and what the company provides to customers or clients. It should also describe the overall goal that employees and executives are pursuing.

2. This is an example of a company's vision statement, which outlines the company's mid- to long-term goals. The vision statement focuses on the market and describes how the company wants to be perceived by the world.

3. This is an example of a values statement. Values statements reflect a company's core values, which reflect what is truly important to the company and form the backbone of its culture.

Review the current situation

Once you've clarified the mission, vision, and values, it's time to review your company's current situation – the second step in defining the strategy. To do this, you examine three things: external influences, internal influences, and the existing strategy. It's important to conduct thorough research in all these areas so you will have a solid understanding of the factors that can affect your strategy.

Reviewing the current situation
External influences

External influences are the macro- and industry-level trends that have an impact on the company's strategy and operations – for instance political, social, or technological factors. You need to assess what's going on in the outside world. This assessment includes the state of the economy, industry growth, prices, regulations, and a general idea of what consumers expect from the company.

The external analysis isn't complete without an assessment of competitors as well. For instance, where do competitors stand in terms of sales and assets? What about profitability and market share?

Internal influences

When you examine internal influences, you consider your own company's performance and capabilities. To do this, you might use a balanced scorecard – a set of performance measures derived from the company's strategy - or rely on financial information to do the assessment.

Another common method for assessing internal influences is to identify the processes required to deliver products and services to customers. The company's goal should be to identify the processes that it can do better or differently to differentiate itself from competitors.

Existing strategy

Examining the existing strategy means identifying the company's existing strengths and weaknesses. Then you summarize the conditions that aren't currently being addressed. These conditions must be addressed when developing the strategy.

Figuring out what a company's strengths and weaknesses are can give it a clear indication of its current situation. A thorough examination of external and internal influences can uncover a lot of information – categorizing it as strengths or weaknesses can help the management team identify the key issues that need to be addressed.

Remember Jarod? He and the rest of his management team are meeting to review the company's current situation. They determine that the biggest external influence on their company is the changing role technology plays in education. When Jarod and his team investigate internal influences, they realize that their technological development process is inferior to that of one of their main competitors. This is an area they definitely want to focus on.

Jarod and his team then examine the company's existing strategy. They find one of the company's key strengths is its high ratings in customer satisfaction surveys.

However, the current strategy doesn't address the technological upgrades required for the company to become one of the top competitors in its industry.

Create strategy direction statements

You've clarified your mission, vision, and values. You have a good idea of your company's current situation. Now you can use that information to create strategy direction statements. This is the third, and final, step in defining your strategy. The information you gleaned during the first two steps is used now to set targets for how the organization intends to create value in the future.

During this step, executives must decide how best to be competitive, and they create their strategy based on these decisions.

Executives have to determine exactly which areas the company will compete in and the direction it will take. What will make the company stand out from competitors? What tasks and processes are needed to accomplish this? Executives should also determine what technology and human capital will be required to execute the strategy.

Strategy formulation usually focuses on customers. However, there are many analysis techniques that are commonly used, and there is no right answer as to which is best to use in different circumstances.

But no matter which technique is used, the most successful companies create strategies based on the market niches they have expertise in. In such niches, they have a solid understanding of customer preferences. Successful companies also know that the key is to set themselves apart from what their competitors are offering. The ultimate goal is to create a sustainable competitive advantage.

The strategy direction statement is what helps executives use all this information to define an executable strategy. To create the direction statement, you must first define the competitive issue, then define the direction statement itself.

Define competitive issue

Defining the competitive issue is all about figuring out where your company stands in terms of competition. Does your company have a specific market niche? Many companies differentiate themselves from competitors by offering something extra. Are you going to give extra value to customers? For instance, perhaps you'll focus on providing exceptional customer service or offering products no one else has.

To define the competitive issue, you must also determine whether your company is, in fact, going to compete with others. Most companies operate in the same market as other companies, but some offer a niche service or product not offered by anyone else.

Define direction statement

Once you've defined the competitive issue, it's time to define the direction statement itself. Each direction statement is like a mini vision statement for each strategic issue and helps to outline what the goals are: the strategic objectives.

It also clarifies the actions the company will have to take to execute the strategy and the measures it will use to monitor the strategy. The direction statements help to create a detailed strategic plan.

For instance, a direction statement for a large university might be, "Our institution will focus our efforts on research and technology. Our aim is to become an industry leader in scientific research among educational institutions. Success will be measured on a bi-annual basis and will be based on our ranking among other educational institutions."

Jarod and his team have already determined that a major strategic challenge is to improve their company's technological development process. Now they need to create strategy direction statements to help them achieve this goal.

Example - See each strategic issue to find out what Jarod and his team came up with for their strategy direction statements.

Improve technology

"Our company's focus is upgrading our technological development process so we can become a top competitor. We will do this by ensuring that our equipment is the best available and that our technicians are the best in their field. Our measure of success will be our position as one of the top five companies in our industry with regard to online sales."

Maintain high customer satisfaction rating

"Our company will focus its efforts on providing individualized service for each of our clients. We will do this by establishing a dedicated team whose sole purpose is to maintain customer relationships. Progress will be monitored by holding monthly meetings between the customer relations team and the executive team."

Case Study
Scenario

Chen is a senior executive at a large national shipping company. She and her team are defining their business strategy for the next five years. Her company prides itself on providing fast, on-time shipping to the entire country, especially the more remote areas. In fact, providing individualized, one-on-one service is one of the most important things in Chen's company. The company hopes to be viewed as a reliable shipper that provides exceptional service.

One of the biggest challenges facing the company is global expansion. Currently, no one in the company has extensive experience with international shipping regulations, and since this is the direction the company wants to go in, it's important that this challenge is addressed.

Right now, the company is very strong in the area of customer service, and it is fairly weak in the area of global development. The company also needs to upgrade its customer database technology because its current program isn't as effective as some other available technology.

Answer the questions in order to help Chen define strategy that executes.

Question

Define the mission, vision, and values for Chen's company by matching each type of statement to its appropriate example.

Options:

A. Mission
B. Vision
C. Values

Targets:

1. "Our company aims to provide fast, reliable shipping to anyone, anywhere."
2. "We want to be one of the top providers of international shipping by the end of the decade."
3. "Our company is committed to customer satisfaction. We are dedicated to providing individualized service."

Answer

Information about the company's aims is found in the mission statement, which describes the company's purpose and what it provides to customers or clients.

Information about the company's vision is found in the vision statement, which outlines the company's mid- to long-term goals. The vision statement focuses on the market and describes how the company wants to be perceived by the world.

Information about the company's values is found in the values statement. Values statements reflect a company's core values, which reflect what is truly important to the company and form the backbone of its culture.

Learning aid - **Defining Strategy**

Defining strategy is the first step in creating executable strategy. To develop a truly focused strategy, you must fully examine the business, its goals, and its environment. Good strategy helps your company build a favorable competitive position. There are three steps involved in defining the strategy.

Step	Description
Clarify the mission, vision, and values	- The mission statement is typically a one- or two-sentence statement that explains your company's purpose - The vision statement outlines the company's mid- to long-term goals - The values statement reflects the company's core values
Review the current situation	- To review the current situation, you examine three things: external influences, internal influences, and the existing strategy - External influences are the macro- and industry-level trends that have an impact on the company's strategy and operations - When you examine internal influences, you consider your own company's performance and capabilities - Examining the existing strategy means identifying the company's existing strengths and weaknesses
Create strategy direction statements	- Executives must decide how best to be competitive, and they formulate strategy based on these decisions - To create the direction statement, you must first define the competitive issue, then define the direction statement itself - Each direction statement must outline the company's activities that make it distinctive and set it apart, the actions it will take to execute the strategy, and potential measures used to monitor and implement the strategy

The critical aspects of strategy

Without a good business strategy, most companies would find it difficult to reach their goals. Strategy development is an essential aspect of execution. There are two aspects of the strategy that can have an effect on its execution. These are the kind of strategy and how it is translated into plans. If you want your strategy to work, you should handle these carefully.

The first aspect is the type of strategy you're executing and how it will affect resources. For instance, a strategy that involves achieving cost leadership, which means driving down the cost of operation, will place demands on the company's resources.

The second aspect of strategy that can affect its execution is the way the strategy is translated into short-term, measurable plans. A company's objectives and performance metrics have to be consistent with its goals and plans.

For instance, if employees don't know how their everyday activities or objectives relate to the business strategy, inconsistencies are inevitable because they won't know why they're working toward a certain goal.

Remember, good execution begins with good strategy. So how can you ensure that your strategy leads to successful execution? You need to take four critical aspects of a strategy into account when developing it. An executable strategy must be planned, integrated, measurable, and supportable.

Critical aspects of strategy

Planned

A realistic, workable strategy begins with good planning. Before you make any major move, evaluate the current situation and possible consequences. Poor planning can significantly affect execution.

Because the goal of business strategy is always to gain competitive advantage, your strategy should be planned to gain an understanding of the industry and competitors, and to develop capabilities that increase your competitive edge.

Integrated

Corporate and business strategies must be integrated if your strategy is to be executed well. The strategies must support each other.

However, several situations can prevent this from happening. For instance, if the corporate and business strategies don't agree on the role of the business, these strategies are unlikely to be achieved.

Measurable

For a business strategy to be executed well, it needs measurable objectives. Everyone involved should know what metrics will be used to measure strategic performance.

You should have a plan in place that can be used to assess your progress with regard to short- and long-term goals.

Supportable

To be successful, the business strategy must be supportable. Trying to make changes that are too big in too short a time could make demands on the organization's skills, resources, and capabilities that can't be supported.

If you ignore these demands, you're unlikely to be able to execute the strategy effectively.

Question

Why is it important to develop strategy that's planned, integrated, measurable, and supportable?

Options:

1. Your strategy will be realistic and workable
2. You'll be able to assess the organization's progress
3. It'll help the organization become competitive
4. It'll help you achieve a clear distinction between corporate and business strategy
5. You'll be able to demonstrate the benefits of making big changes quickly

Answer

Option 1: This option is correct. Your strategy will be realistic and workable if you employ good planning. This means evaluating the current situation and possible consequences before you make any major move.

Option 2: This option is correct. Measurable objectives will ensure that you're able to assess the organization's progress. For a strategy to be executed well, it needs metrics used to measure strategic performance. You need a plan in place that can be used to assess your progress with regard to short- and long-term goals.

Option 3: This option is correct. The goal of business strategy is to gain competitive advantage. Your strategy should be well planned to gain an understanding of the industry and competitors, and to develop capabilities that increase your competitive edge.

Option 4: This option is incorrect. Actually, a strategy that's executed well is integrated, which means that corporate and business strategies must support each other.

Option 5: This option is incorrect. To be successful, the business strategy must be supportable. Trying to make changes that are too big in too short a time could make demands on the organization's skills, resources, and capabilities that can't be supported.

Selecting strategic initiatives

You've already learned that the first step in creating your business strategy is to define the strategy. Now it's time to move on to the second step in creating strategy that executes: develop the strategy.

Developing the strategy involves four steps:
- select strategic initiatives based on themes,
- assign accountability to initiatives,
- translate initiatives into strategic targets, and
- allocate resources to initiatives.

The first step in developing a strategy involves actually selecting strategic initiatives. Not all strategies should be implemented. It's important to evaluate which strategies you should choose to implement, based on the existing situation in your company and the potential consequences.

Poor planning can negatively affect many areas of the organization – for instance you could fail to obtain needed resources. Sound planning and a clear, focused strategy are essential if the company is to reach its goals.

That's where strategic initiatives come in. They're the short-term actions that guide your company toward achieving its vision. The company screens strategic initiatives and selects them by examining whether they help the company achieve its objectives.

Selecting strategic initiatives involves five steps. First, you examine the strategic objectives that have arisen from the direction statements. Next, you cluster the objectives into strategic "themes." Themes are what the organization wants to accomplish and focus on for the future. Third, you create a strategy map, which essentially showcases the organization's goals and how these will be achieved. Next, you need to assign performance measures and, finally, choose your initiatives.

Strategic initiatives

Examine strategic objectives

During the defining process, you will have formulated strategic objectives in each of the four strategy map perspectives: financial, customer, internal, and learning and growth. The objectives are the continuous improvement activities that link to your strategic themes.

Your objectives will vary in each of the four perspectives. An example of a healthcare company's objectives in the customer perspective might be to build ten new strategic alliances annually and to establish an international CRM process. The company's financial perspective might include an objective of "to expand sales to Asian customers by 25% in five years."

Cluster objectives into themes

The strategic themes subdivide the overall business strategy into logical and manageable linked objectives. The merit of using themes is that they cross functions and departments and so support the all-encompassing approach required for good strategy execution.

The chief customer officer at the healthcare company could group the customer objectives under the theme "Grow customer base."

Create a strategy map

A strategy map is a one-page visual representation of all the strategic themes, or clusters of objectives, you identified. The map allows you to match themes to objectives and assign the appropriate leadership.

The objectives are linked in cause-effect relationships to produce a strategy map for each strategic theme. Upward pointing arrows link the objectives to indicate either cause and effect or strategic support.

To create a map, you need to define how you will evaluate the success of the objective by identifying measures. You then list the actions that are needed in order to complete each objective, thus reaching your initiatives.

Assign performance measures

While that strategy map provides a clarification of objectives and how they interconnect across the organization to achieve strategy, making strategy actionable is achieved by assigning performance measures to each strategic objective. Measures are parameters that help you assess progress toward meeting the objective.

You need to define clear measures that will enable you to improve your business. The priority is to focus on quantifiable factors that are directly linked to strategic objectives. These are known as key performance indicators, or KPIs.

List actions and choose initiatives

You now list the actions that are required to achieve each of your strategic objectives. These actions are your initiatives and ensure success of the business.

Initiatives associated with any one objective should not be considered out of context. Achieving a strategic objective usually requires multiple and complementary initiatives from various parts of the organization – across the four strategy map perspectives.

Example - Jarod, who is a manager at an international educational book retailer, has found that his company's technology needs have changed. In order to address the needs of customers, he has to make some major changes to the way his company sells online in order to remain competitive.

With his management team, he determines that some key strategic objectives are to increase customer loyalty and retention and maintain outstanding customer service. These objectives relate to a financial objective of increasing gross profit by 10% annually. An internal objective of executing a web-enabled CRM, or customer relationship management, program and a learning and growth objective of developing a broad set of skills to support customers support the objectives. He clusters all the objectives into a new theme – Improve Customer Experience – and creates his strategy map for this theme.

The next thing Jarod does is identify the measures for each objective. The first objective is to increase customer loyalty and retention. This can be measured by ascertaining the number of return customers to the web site. The second objective is to maintain outstanding customer service. This can be measured in a number of different ways – for example by keeping track of the number of complaints from customers about products or average order-fulfillment times.

Jarod lists the actions that are required to complete each Customer objective. See each Customer objective to find out what Jarod decides are the actions required.

Increase customer loyalty and retention

Jarod determines that improving turnaround time is vital. He thinks increasing the number of warehouse staff who pack orders would solve the problem.

Jarod establishes that a personalized, customizable online site would draw back customers and encourage them to purchase more by using the automated recommendations. He also establishes a "thank-you" service to top customers by offering them 10% off online merchandise for a period of time.

Maintain outstanding customer service

Jarod decides that implementing a new online ordering system would help maintain customer service. He also initiates an internal employee reward program for those with the best feedback from customers. He knows also that executing a web-enabled CRM program will go a long way to maintaining customer service.

So your company's executives have selected a number of initiatives. What comes next? Now, the initiatives are evaluated and ranked by scoring according to company-specific criteria.

Examples of these criteria include strategic fit, resource requirements, and risk, to name just a few.

After considering the initiatives, Jarod's company determines that the most imperative ones are the online thank-you service and the employee reward program.

These two initiatives have minimal risk and a potentially large return on investment.

Question

Chen is a senior executive at a large national shipping company. She and her team are developing their strategy and have determined that a key strategic direction is to focus their efforts on creating a global shipping department. Chen and her team have now moved on to the initial development stages and are selecting strategic initiatives. They have reviewed the two strategic objectives associated with this direction: "implement storage facilities" and "expand haulage fleet to 100 trailers within 6 months."

How should Chen and her team best go about selecting strategic initiatives based on themes?

Options:

1. Cluster the objectives into the theme of "Global shipping enterprise" and assign performance measures to the strategic objectives

2. Create a strategy map that outlines not only the global shipping enterprise theme, but all the themes and objectives identified

3. Determine that two of their themes will be to create a global shipping department and to enhance their database technology

4. Decide that their company's mission is to provide fast, reliable shipping to customers across the country

5. Select initiatives of "build a 500,000 square foot covered warehouse for transit and long-term storage" and "acquire 100 modern trailers"

Answer

Option 1: This option is correct. When you're selecting strategic initiatives based on themes, you must actually develop the strategic themes. Achieving objectives in one area of the organization usually entails complementary initiatives from other parts of the company. Grouping them into themes is a good way to see how objectives relate to each other.

Option 2: This option is correct. When you're selecting strategic initiatives based on themes, you need to create a strategy map. This is a one-page visual representation of all the strategic themes you identified.

Option 3: This option is incorrect. Actually, the company should create its objectives, not the themes, based on these strategies.

Option 4: This option is incorrect. This is actually an example of the company's mission statement. It isn't something that is done when selecting strategic initiatives based on themes.

Option 5: This option is correct. The final step is to list the actions that are required to achieve each of your strategic objectives. These actions are your initiatives and ensure success of the business.

Assigning accountability

Once you've selected strategic initiatives based on themes, the next step is to assign accountability to the initiatives. This basically means deciding who owns the themes and assigning a group of individuals to execute the tasks associated with them.

Strategic themes require strong leadership to ensure they are assigned adequate resources and are visible within the company. Therefore, usually one or two executives, called theme owners, are assigned to each strategic theme so it will get the necessary attention. They're responsible for leading a team of individuals who will execute tasks associated with the theme. They're also in charge of assessing execution of the theme's strategic objectives, identifying key issues, and sponsoring new initiatives or changes.

Example - See each of the theme owner's responsibilities to learn more about it.

Leading a team

Each theme owner leads a team, which is a group of employees taken from various business and support units who are responsible for executing the tasks associated with the theme.

Assessing execution of the theme's strategic objectives

The theme owner is responsible for assessing the execution of the themes across the whole company.

Identifying key issues

The theme owner identifies key issues that affect strategic implementation and suggests actions that might be appropriate as well as who should be accountable.

Sponsoring initiatives or changes

The theme owner is responsible for sponsoring initiatives or changes to existing initiatives as well as ensuring that the proposed changes are on the agenda for management to examine.

The team members are chosen because of their strengths and expertise. They don't have authority over business functions, but they do have certain responsibilities. The team's first job is to link the theme's strategic objectives to operations.

The team also determines who is to complete each initiative. Sometimes, an existing organizational unit will be assigned an initiative. Other times, however, the team will have to hand over responsibility to a project management office that has experience with large-scale projects.

Both the theme owner and team must monitor the performance of all the theme's initiatives. If any initiative isn't executed properly, the whole strategic theme could be in danger of failure. Theme owners and teams should meet regularly to review progress and ensure everyone is on track.

Example - Jarod at the educational book publisher knows the importance of assigning strong leadership to each strategic theme. For the "Improve Customer Experience" theme, he chooses Michael, a senior customer service executive to be the theme owner.

Michael chooses a dedicated experienced team of individuals to work with him. They'll be responsible for taking care of all the tasks associated with executing the theme, so he selects people whom he knows can meet the challenge.

Question

Chen has selected the theme "Global shipping enterprise" to encompass her team's objectives. She and her team have determined that the initiatives will be to build a 500,000 square foot covered warehouse and to acquire 100 modern trailers. She assigns accountability to Tracey, head of operations, whom she selects to be the theme owner.

What should Tracey and her theme team do to ensure they fulfill their roles?

Options:

1. Tracey and her theme team monitor the building and trailer acquisition initiatives

2. Tracey evaluates achievement of the objectives associated with creating the global shipping enterprise companywide

3. The theme team creates an action plan for teams based on customer service strategies

4. The theme team identifies an issue with a vendor that could affect strategic implementation of the acquisition initiative

5. Tracey determines who is to complete each of the two initiatives

Answer

Option 1: This option is correct. Both the theme owner and theme team are responsible for monitoring the performance of all the theme's initiatives. The whole strategic theme could be in danger if any initiative isn't executed properly.

Option 2: This option is correct. The theme owner is responsible for assessing the execution of the theme's cross-functional strategic objectives across the whole company.

Option 3: This option is correct. The theme owner identifies key issues that affect strategic implementation, suggests actions that might be appropriate, and advises on who should be accountable.

Option 4: This option is incorrect. It's actually the theme owner, not the team, who identifies key issues that affect strategic implementation.

Option 5: This option is incorrect. It's actually the theme team, not the theme owner, who determines who is to complete each initiative.

Learning aid - **Develop the Strategy**

The second step in creating strategy that executes, which is to develop the strategy, involves performing four key steps.

Step	Description
Select strategic initiatives based on themes	- Not all strategies should be implemented; you must evaluate which strategies you should choose to implement, based on the existing situation in your company and the potential consequences - First, develop strategic objectives by deciding on the short-term or long-term change you want to accomplish - Next, develop strategic themes, which are clusters of related objectives - Finally, create a strategy map, which is a one-page visual representation of all the strategic themes, or clusters of objectives
Assign accountability to initiatives	- The next step is to assign accountability to the initiatives by deciding who owns the themes and assigning theme teams to execute the portfolios - The theme owner assesses execution of the theme's strategic objectives, identifies key issues, and sponsors initiatives or changes - The theme team links strategic objectives to operations and determines who is to complete each initiative - Both the theme owner and the theme team monitor the performance of all the theme's objectives
Translating initiatives into strategic targets	- Strategic targets are the short-term operational metrics that are linked directly to a company's long-term needs - Before setting a target, you must ensure three things: that it's essential for success, that the organizational capability is present to achieve it, and that the necessary workforce motivation is there to accept the challenge
Allocating resources to initiatives	- Strategy places demands on resources, and you need to direct your company's strategy by managing resource allocation - You do this by knowing your people and their capabilities, ensuring that managers evaluate the strategy, and connecting the business units

From initiatives to strategic targets

When you're developing an executable strategy, you need to take four key steps. You've already learned about the first two – selecting strategic initiatives based on themes and assigning accountability to initiatives. Now it's time to move on to the final two steps, which are translating initiatives into strategic targets and allocating resources to initiatives.

Successful execution depends on how well you translate the initiatives into strategic targets. These targets are the short-term operational metrics that are linked directly to your company's long-term needs. If you want to achieve the long-term goals, you must manage the short-term targets well.

You've ascertained what measures are associated with each of the strategic objectives. It's now time to assign targets to these measures. Setting performance targets gives everyone in the organization a clear picture of what they should be aiming for.

The balanced scorecard is a strategic planning and management tool that's used to monitor performance against goals. It allows you to balance the targets to be measured over the four key areas of financials, customer service, internal business processes, and learning and growth.

The balanced scorecard complements financial measures of past performance by providing additional measures of future performance. Essentially, it helps you translate the strategy map objectives into actionable targets.

Target setting begins with the vision statement when an executive sets a high-level target. This target then creates a value gap between the aspiration and the current reality. The strategy must close this gap.

Targets are reached by splitting the value gap established at the highest level into logically consistent targets for customer, process, and learning and growth metrics.

Targets will be specific to your organization, but could include reduced wait time, increased customer satisfaction, process improvement, or cost savings.

When you're setting targets, you may want to consider several areas. These include employees; national, state, local, or industry averages; trends and baselines; other agencies; and feedback.

Employees

Employees are usually the people in your organization who are closest to the action, and they can often provide the best insight into what makes a good target.

National, state, local, or industry averages

If your company monitors the performance of government and nonprofit agencies, this can be a good source of potential target information.

Trends and baselines

When you're setting a performance target, you should examine current results on the metric, or how things are performing right now. Past data and trends can help you choose a target that provides a meaningful, yet realistic, challenge.

Other agencies

Although some private-sector firms might be unwilling to share information, public and nonprofit companies are usually happy to share and learn from each other.

Feedback

Asking customers and other stakeholders for feedback about your company can be a great way to set targets.

Targets can be difficult to assign. You can use two techniques when setting targets to close the value gap.

The first technique involves splitting the overall value gap into targets for each strategic theme. Basically, you determine if the target can be divided into subtargets, relating to the four perspectives that strategic themes are based on: customer, process, financial, and learning and growth.

Then you use the second technique, which is to divide the subtargets for each strategic theme into strategic objectives, making sure that the objectives all relate back to the original high-level target.

For example, suppose a bank wants to increase its operating income from $20 million to $100 million over the next five years. This creates a value gap. Closing this value gap requires that the initiative be divided among four perspectives: process, financial, customer, and learning and growth.

Example - See each perspective to learn how the bank closes the value gap.

Process perspective

For the process perspective, the bank sets a subtarget to reduce the cost of serving each customer by 25%.

Financial perspective

For the financial perspective, the bank sets a subtarget to raise revenue by 50% per customer.

Customer perspective

For the customer perspective, the bank sets a subtarget to attract 400,000 new customers.

Learning and growth perspective

For the learning and growth perspective, the bank will implement a training program to ensure all customer service representatives are knowledgeable in all processing techniques.

Once you've determined your subtargets, you can break them down into objectives that relate back to the high-level target you previously set.

For instance, for its financial perspective subtarget to raise revenue by 50% per customer, the bank identifies its objective is to increase customer retention by providing higher levels of personal service.

This will require that the learning and growth perspective have a subtarget of increasing staff members' competency so they'll know how to handle the personal service. This subtarget can be broken down into the objective of reducing the departure of high-quality employees.

You'll know that targets align with objectives if achieving them allows your company to close its value gap and achieve the goal of the vision. Before setting a target, you must ensure three things: that it's essential for success, that the organizational capability is present to achieve it, and that the necessary workforce motivation is there to accept the challenge.

Setting targets

Essential for success

Is the target truly essential for your company's success? If employees think the target is just wishful thinking by managers, they will likely be skeptical about their ability to achieve it.

For instance, suppose a company's management team decides to have a stretch target of zero customer complaints. The team's thinking behind this is that it has noticed a dramatic decline in customer complaints since implementing an online help and support program. This target might be unrealistic and not really critical to the company's success because there is already such a noticeable decline in complaints.

Organizational capability

Is your organization actually able to achieve the target? Capability is made up of vital resources such as funding, employee skills, knowledgeable management, IT systems, and human capital.

Without the organizational capability needed to support the target, many companies simply fail to meet their goals.

For example, the organization's capability might not lend itself to zero customer complaints. Because the company develops innovative software programs, it would be impossible to be completely free of bugs for the version of new software programs.

Necessary workforce motivation

Does your company have the workforce motivation in place that's needed to accept the challenge? If employees aren't motivated to achieve the target, they probably won't put in the effort required to meet the goal.

For instance, the company's employees might not buy into this target because if only one customer complains, they would feel that they have failed to meet the target.

There are as many different types of targets as there are organizations that create them. For instance, suppose a large insurance company wants to reduce by ten days the amount of time customers must wait before receiving their claims.

Implementing this change will require that the company purchases an expensive new computer system so employees can process customer claims faster.

Before going ahead with the change, the insurance company executives consider the criteria for setting targets.

First, they ask themselves if it's essential for the company's success. Their answer – yes – is based on the fact that the company has been losing its competitive advantage as it deals with a backlog of claims.

Next they consider whether the company has the organizational capability to achieve the target. The resources are there, both in terms of finances and number of employees.

Finally, they consider employee motivation. Employees have been complaining recently about having to deal with unhappy customers. So the executives are certain the employees are motivated to learn the new system.

Question

Chen is a senior executive at a large national shipping company. She and her team have already selected two initiatives to execute and are now translating these into strategic targets.

Their key strategic initiatives are to build a 500,000 square foot covered warehouse and to acquire 100 modern trailers. Currently, her company is a leader in national shipping, but to remain competitive, it's essential that it moves to a more global focus.

For the past few months, the HR Department has been preparing to interview and hire new staff. The entire company is ready to embrace the change, and employees are optimistic about the changes. They're willing to work hard to make the new warehouse a reality.

Which strategic targets are appropriate for this company?

Options:

1. Build a 10,000 square foot warehouse for a new global shipping department by the end of the quarter
2. Have new database ready to go with all employees trained to use it by the end of the month
3. Reduce staff numbers by 10% in order to become a more significant global competitor
4. Increase national sales by 25% over the next five years

Answer

Option 1: This option is correct. The qualities of a good target are that it's essential for success, the company has organizational capability to handle it, and the workforce is

Business Execution

motivated to achieve it. Because all of these are present in Chen's company, building a 10,000 square foot warehouse is a realistic target.

Option 2: This option is correct. Having a new database ready to go by the end of the month is a realistic target for Chen's company because all of the necessary factors are present: it's essential for success, the organizational capability is present, and the workforce is motivated.

Option 3: This option is incorrect. Hiring new staff is essential to the success of the initiative, so reducing staff isn't a realistic target for Chen's company.

Option 4: This option is incorrect. Chen's company isn't focusing on the national market; it's trying to break into the global market. Therefore, increasing national sales isn't a realistic target.

Allocate resources to initiatives

The final step in developing strategy involves allocating resources to initiatives. This places demands on a company's skills, resources, and capabilities. Resource allocation must align strictly with overall strategy.

Once you've established a strategy, it's important that you don't make drastic changes because your company might not be able to support them in the short term.

It's also important that each of the company's departmental capabilities is in line with the overall strategy and are able to support it.

Because strategy places demands on resources, you need to manage resource allocation. You do this by knowing your people and their capabilities, ensuring that managers evaluate the strategy, and connecting the departments.

Allocating resources
Knowing people and their capabilities

When you're allocating resources to initiatives, you need to know the people whose names appear on the proposals. Resources can be scarce, and it's important to know the track records of the people sponsoring proposals. If they have good implementation records, then there's probably not much risk in approving the initiatives.

For instance, the manager of the business units responsible for processing insurance claims must be confident that his team has the skills and proficiencies necessary to process claims quickly.

Ensuring managers evaluate the strategy

You should make sure managers evaluate the strategy itself. Instead of evaluating whether the proposal is the best way to implement an initiative, managers should spend time discussing whether they should support the business idea at all.

For example, the manager must evaluate whether or not his department has the necessary resources, such as enough people to reduce claim times. If not, he might need to put more people on the job.

Connecting the departments

Managers need to know how resource allocation affects the entire company. Try to frame questions about resource allocation so they connect up departments. Asking "what's best for the company?" can be especially important in cases where large amounts of money are involved or when multiple departments are involved in the initiative being considered.

For instance, managers must understand how reducing claim times will affect the overall organization. Reducing claim wait times might decrease customer complaints, which in turn affects the company's reputation, making it a more desirable insurance company.

Resources – both in terms of people and funding – have to be provided for every strategic theme's portfolio of initiatives. Typically, you use a top-down process to establish funding levels to determine the quantity of resources for each theme. You also use a bottom-up process to select the specific initiatives that are to receive the funding.

So where does funding come from for the business strategy? There should be only one level of funding to support each strategic initiative. Say you need to train a group of employees in a new software package. The funding shouldn't come from the HR training funds, because then the initiative will be competing for money with other training projects.

Even with targeted funding – where each initiative has its own pool of funding – sometimes theme owners require more money.

For example, if a theme owner can convince executives that a portfolio of initiatives will yield higher performance or revenues for the company, the case can often be made to increase spending.

Question

Chen and her team have decided to go ahead and submit a proposal for their initiatives of creating a new global shipping department and upgrading their customer database.

How can Chen effectively manage resource allocation for her strategy?

Options:

1. She chooses people with proven track records to write the proposal

2. She ensures that managers spend time discussing the initiatives to be certain they're the best strategies

3. She demonstrates how implementing the two initiatives will help not only the Sales Department, but the entire company

4. She asks for volunteers to write the proposal, and decides to go with the person who seems the most knowledgeable

5. She determines which business unit will be most impacted by the initiatives, and assigns the majority of the funds to it

Answer

Option 1: This option is correct. When you're allocating resources to initiatives, it's important to know the people whose names appear on the proposals. When resources are scarce, you should know the track records of the people sponsoring proposals.

Option 2: This option is correct. When allocating resources, ensure that managers evaluate the strategy itself, and not whether the proposal is the best way to implement the initiative.

Option 3: This option is correct. When you're allocating resources, it's important to show managers how resource allocation affects the entire company.

Option 4: This option is incorrect. When you're allocating resources, you need to base your decisions on proven track records, and not just go with whoever seems the most knowledgeable.

Option 5: This option is incorrect. Managers need to know how resource allocation affects the entire company, not just one or two departments or units.

CHAPTER THREE
Linking Strategy to People and Operations

The importance of communicating strategy

All too often, organizations create well-formulated strategies that appear to take every contingency into account, but fail to get the desired results. On paper, your organization may have a brilliant plan. Without the right business execution, however, this plan can often fail to turn your vision into a reality. Why is it that companies fail to implement their plans effectively? One key reason may be because they don't clearly communicate their strategic goals to employees.

Before communicating your organization's strategy, you need to fully understand that strategy and your employees.

Business execution depends on getting the right people to perform the tasks that are critical to your strategy. This involves assigning activities to employees with the right mix of skills and abilities to carry the activities out effectively.

You must also communicate the goals of the strategy. You need to link these goals to your employees' personal goals, and ensure they understand how their work contributes to the success of the strategy.

Question

In some organizations, the workforce may be unaware of what strategy the company is trying to implement. A lack of effective communication can lead some employees to believe the strategy applies only to senior managers.

How effective do you think your organization is at communicating its strategies?

Options:
1. Very effective
2. Somewhat effective
3. Not at all effective

Answer

Option 1: You said that your organization is very effective in communicating strategies – that's great! Being able to communicate your company's strategy helps employees see how their work is aligned with the organization's goals.

Option 2: You say that your organization is somewhat effective in communicating its strategy. Increasing your knowledge of communicating strategy may improve the outcome of your organization's strategic goals.

Option 3: You note that your organization is not at all effective at communicating its strategy. To ensure that your organization's strategy is implemented successfully, it's critical that you communicate your plan effectively to all levels of employees.

Communicating strategy is important for three reasons. First, employees need to understand how their tasks fit into the big picture. Second, for a strategy to be executed, it must be translated into individual tasks and assigned to the appropriate people. Communicating strategy will require you to do this. And finally, employees are more likely to be motivated if they know how their roles relate to the organization's goals.

Communicating new directions or strategies is often overlooked in companies. However, this is a key task in ensuring your organizational plans are executed properly.

Even the most well-organized plan is unlikely to succeed if those who implement it either don't know about the plan or misunderstand it.

That's why informing employees about your strategy and providing them with relevant information is key to the successful implementation of your organization's strategy.

Question

Why do you think it's important to communicate your organization's plan to ensure its successful execution?

Options:

1. It can help employees to become more committed to your organization's goals

2. It allows you to focus on the employees who have the biggest influence in defining your organization's strategy

3. It requires you to convert the company's strategy into actionable tasks for individual employees

4. It helps employees recognize how their tasks are linked to the company's goal

5. It allows your organization to adapt its strategy depending on your employees' capabilities

Answer

Option 1: This option is correct. If employees understand how their tasks relate to the company's larger goals, they're more likely to become engaged by their work.

Option 2: This option is incorrect. When communicating your organization's strategy, you need to inform all members of your company's workforce, from senior management to frontline staff, so that actions and decisions are coordinated.

Option 3: This option is correct. Effective communication of organizational strategy involves translating your plan into individual priorities and goals that can help to execute your organization's plan better.

Option 4: This option is correct. To increase motivation and commitment to the organization's goal, employees should be able to see the big picture and how they fit into it.

Option 5: This option is incorrect. Organizational strategies should already be aligned to employees' particular skills and shouldn't have to be changed during the business execution process.

Mission, values, vision, and strategy

Before communicating strategies to employees, you first need to consider your organization's mission, values, and vision. These concepts are central to most companies. They can inspire employees and help to focus decisions on the customers' needs. For an organization to move forward, everyone involved must have a common understanding of the direction the company is taking.

Your company's mission, values, and vision statements are central to its strategy. The mission statement defines your organization's purpose. The values statement describes its most important guiding principles. And the vision statement outlines the results it hopes to realize, as well as its future aspirations. These concepts should be reviewed on an ongoing basis to create a plan of action that can help your organization adapt to new global trends.

For example, take Juan, the chief operations officer at a large multinational electronics company. Juan and several other senior managers are trying to devise a new strategy for their organization to help overcome a recent drop in sales. They first clarify their mission statement: "To provide high-quality and innovative products worldwide supported by exceptional customer service."

Juan also reviews the values statement: "We want to anticipate our customers' needs and revive their sense of wonder in new products." Finally, Juan and his colleagues consider their organization's vision statement: "To be one of the top three global electronics manufacturers within the next five years."

With these statements in mind, Juan and his colleagues create a new organizational strategy: "To strengthen our geographic focus on growing overseas markets in Asia and Africa."

Question

Imagenie is an advertising agency that's outlined mission, values, and vision statements to help influence its future strategies.

Match each statement to the corresponding statement type.

Options:

A. "To provide top-quality advertising campaigns that reach target audiences and meet our clients' objectives"

B. "We are a client-driven agency that's committed to excellence, accountability, and value for money" C. "To double revenue from online advertisements within the next three years"

Targets:

1. Mission statement
2. Values statement
3. Vision statement

Answer

A mission statement outlines why the company exists. For example, a company's mission might be to reach key target audiences and meet clients' objectives.

A values statement describes what a company considers to be the most important factors underpinning its strategies and processes. For instance, an organization's values statement might be concerned with accountability and value for money.

A vision statement defines a company's mid- to long-term goals. For example, a company's vision might be to increase its sales figures within a specific period of time.

Principles for communicating strategy

Having developed a strategy based on your mission, values, and vision statements, you then communicate this strategy by applying several important principles. First you explain the reason behind this strategy, not just what the strategy is. You need to communicate constantly using multiple methods. You have to get involved with the employees who execute the strategy, and make employees understand the benefits of the decision. Finally, you must communicate in ways that invite employee participation in shaping your organization's strategy.

The first principle to apply when communicating your organization's new strategy is to explain the reason behind the strategy. Remember that it's not enough just to provide details about what actions your company is going to take or describe employees' new responsibilities.

When communicating new strategies to employees, you have to point out what has motivated management to make this decision. You could point to changing marketplace trends, low sales figures, or new regulations or technology as key factors in the decision.

For instance, suppose your organization's plan is to merge with another company. You might explain that sales revenues have been falling and the merger will help your organization increase its market share.

Keep in mind that without an honest explanation of your organization's new strategy, employees may react negatively to the decision. Rumors about the strategy might soon spread, and employees may make up their own reasons for the strategy.

Remember Juan? Having outlined his company's new strategy, he decides to create a communication plan to inform employees of the strategy.

In the plan, he explains that the organization is facing extensive competition in the North American and European markets. He points out that, as a result, the company has experienced a drop in sales in the last three quarters.

He also explains that the Asian and African markets represent a major opportunity for his organization to grow and take on some of its main rivals.

Question

Martha is a senior project manager at a pharmaceutical company. Her company has decided to restructure and decentralize its research and development unit.

Which statement best explains the reason for this strategy?

Options:

1. "Our company needs to reduce spending, and by spreading our R&D unit out globally, we can take advantage of cheaper labor costs"

2. "Creating a collaborative R&D network across the globe will support the development of innovation management for our future growth"

3. "Many of our main competitors are improving their productivity by adopting a strategy of expanding and distributing R&D units worldwide"

Answer

Option 1: This is the correct option. This statement highlights a need to cut costs as one of the main reasons the company is adopting the new strategy.

Option 2: This option is incorrect. This statement outlines one of the possible benefits of the new strategy, but doesn't describe the root cause of the decision.

Option 3: This option is incorrect. The fact that the strategy has been adopted by another organization doesn't explain why Martha's company should also use this strategy.

The second principle when communicating your organization's strategy is to communicate constantly using multiple methods. To ensure your employees fully understand the strategy, you must repeat your organization's message frequently. An effective way of doing this is to use different communication media and formats, including presentations, newsletters, posters, meetings, local intranet sites, and training programs. To check your employees' understanding, you could periodically ask them to explain in their own words what your organization's new plan is.

The third principle for communicating strategy is to get involved with the employees who execute the strategy. As a leader, you need to ensure that your organization's strategy is linked to the frontline staff whose tasks can make the plan a reality.

Leaders involved in high-level planning and strategic thinking often overlook how the plan will be implemented. They may have a strategic vision for the organization, but fail to translate their vision into specific tasks.

To execute your organization's strategy, you need to become personally involved with all the people who will affect the outcome. You must define tasks and priorities for your workforce, and collaborate with key stakeholders.

For example, if your aim is to increase your organization's range of products, you could work closely with the Sales or Marketing Departments to create a targeted marketing plan.

Consider Juan again. To ensure his employees understand the new strategy, he first organizes a meeting where all staff members are present. At the meeting, he outlines details of his organization's plan to focus on emerging markets, and then invites questions from the audience.

He then follows up on the meeting by circulating a weekly newsletter that provides insights into the Asian and African markets.

And as part of his organization's strategy, Juan collaborates closely with manufacturers and suppliers within the key markets to analyze shipping and other logistical issues.

Question

Match each example action to the corresponding principle for communicating strategy. Each principle may have more than one match.

Options:

A. Ben consults staff in the Sales Department about a new pricing strategy to find out where savings can be made

B. Chen sets up a training course as well as an intranet site to help employees deal with a strategy to diversify company services

C. Tom updates a bulletin board and holds monthly IT reviews so his company can double its number of applications

D. Omar agrees on a schedule with the R&D Department to enable his company to accelerate product launches

Targets:

1. Communicate constantly using multiple methods
2. Communicate with those who execute strategy

Answer

Chen and Tom's actions both relate to communicating their organizations' strategies using different methods.

Ben and Omar's actions involve communicating with key stakeholders who can help their companies execute their strategies.

The next principle is to make sure employees understand the benefits of the new corporate strategy. In general, organizational strategies tend to focus on the benefits for the company and its clients. But your strategy should also consider possible benefits for the employees who will execute the plan.

Example - See each type of benefit for more information.

Benefits for company and clients

Outlining the benefits for your company and its customers can motivate your employees.

You could, for example, explain how improved processes can increase sales, reduce costs, and stop project overruns. You might also point out how the strategy will improve the organization's functions and ensure better customer service.

Benefits for employees

Explaining the benefits for your workforce is essential for employee engagement. And providing performance-related incentives is one way of getting employees to support your organization's strategy.

For instance, if your strategy requires staff members to complete training, you could point out that they'll develop personally and increase their chances for promotion.

Other incentives may include greater company share options or improved bonus schemes that may be implemented as part of the strategy.

The final principle is to communicate in ways that invite employee participation in shaping the organization's strategy. If employees have a greater say in the execution of the strategy, they're more likely to feel like part of the process and support it.

Two-way communication enables employees to question the strategy and ask for clarification. This helps them get a better understanding of the strategy, which can motivate them to support it.

Inviting employee participation can also make your strategy more effective. By using feedback from frontline staff, you can find out what is and isn't working and change the strategy accordingly.

For example, you could set up one-on-one meetings and group sessions with management where employees can provide feedback on the strategy. An online suggestion box could allow employees to submit ideas for changes to the strategy. Or you might carry out surveys to gauge employees' level of commitment and motivation for the new strategy.

To explain the benefits of the new strategy, Juan organizes several staff meetings where he outlines how the organization will be able to increase sales and dominate the market share in the new regions.

He also points out that with increased revenue, there will be better prospects for promotion and possible increases in salary.

Juan then designs a survey where employees are asked how their work can impact the strategy and how important their contributions are.

Question

Carol is the chief communications officer at a multinational merchandise retail company. The company has recently decided to enter the cell phone market, and it's Carol's responsibility to communicate this strategy to the employees.

Match each of Carol's actions to the corresponding principle for communicating strategies.

Options:

A. She explains to employees that the company's retail market is contracting and that diversifying its product range represents an opportunity for growth

B. She sets up an intranet site, and creates a number of posters describing the strategy, posting them in conference rooms, staff kitchens, and employee workstations

C. She consults with executives in the Marketing Department to devise a new advertising campaign highlighting the company's new service

Targets:
1. Explain reason behind strategy
2. Communicate constantly using multiple methods
3. Get involved with those who execute strategy

Answer

By pointing out the need to expand the company's range of services, Carol is explaining the main reason for the organization's new strategy.

By using an extensive poster campaign, Carol can communicate the strategy to employees on an ongoing basis.

Carol links the successful execution of the company's strategy with the staff members whose tasks will have the biggest effect on it – the Marketing Department.

Question

Match each of Carol's actions to the corresponding principle for communicating strategies.

Options:

A. She points out that with diversified services, the company can expect market share growth, and that employees may get bonuses if targets are reached

B. She organizes a weekly staff meeting to get feedback from employees about how the new telephone service should be advertised

Targets:

1. Make employees understand benefits
2. Invite employee participation

Answer

By outlining some of the advantages, such as market share growth and bonuses, Carol helps employees understand the benefits of the strategy for themselves and the company.

Carol tries to get buy-in from the employees by inviting them to participate in shaping the strategy by making suggestions about advertising.

Learning aid - **Principles for Communicating Strategy**

Successful implementation of your organization's strategy depends on effective communication between leaders and employees. Review the different principles and actions involved, and consider whether your company is applying them.

Business Execution

Principles	Actions
Explain reason behind strategy	Describe the motivation behind the strategy by pointing out important factors, such as changing marketplace trends or low sales figures
	Provide an honest explanation of your organization's new strategy to prevent inaccurate information from spreading throughout your workforce
Communicate constantly using multiple methods	Repeat your organization's message frequently by using different communication media and formats such as presentations, newsletters, posters, meetings, local intranet sites, and training programs
	Check your employees' understanding by periodically asking them to explain in their own words what your organization's new plan is
Get involved with those who execute the strategy	Define tasks and priorities for your workforce, and collaborate closely with key stakeholders
Make employees understand the benefits of the decision	Explain how the strategy can help your organization by, for example, improving processes, increasing sales, reducing costs, or ensuring better customer service
	Motivate your employees by providing performance-related incentives, such as greater company share options or improved bonus schemes
	Point out that employees will develop personally and increase their chances for promotion by taking on greater responsibilities or by completing training required as part of the new strategy
Communicate in ways that invite employee participation in shaping the strategy	Use feedback from frontline staff to find out if your strategy is working effectively and to change it accordingly
	Set up one-on-one meetings and group sessions with management where employees can provide feedback on the strategy
	Provide an online suggestion box so employees can submit ideas for changes to the strategy
	Carry out employee surveys to gauge their level of commitment and motivation for the new strategy

Purpose of balanced scorecards

Suppose you've created a strategy based on your company's mission, values, and vision statements. And suppose you've communicated this strategy to your employees so they understand and support the plan. How do you then translate your strategy into action and ensure your employees execute their tasks effectively? One possible method is to use a balanced scorecard, or BSC.

The BSC is a performance management process that can help you monitor your employees' objectives and ensure their tasks align with your organization's goals.

It can be used to convert an organization's strategy from a passive document into an effective plan of action that departments, teams, and individuals can use on a daily basis.

The balanced scorecard also provides a framework for measuring an organization's activities and employees' individual performances to find out if they're truly reaching the company's strategic goals.

BSCs can also be used to align processes within an organization. When business units work in isolation, goals and processes can sometimes become misaligned, slowing the progress of your strategy. To avoid these disconnected practices, your organization needs to achieve synergy across four scorecard perspectives: financial, customer, process, and learning and growth. Each perspective contains its own set of objectives and measures which can then be extended organization-wide.

See each perspective of balanced scorecards for more information.

Financial perspective

The financial perspective relates to how shareholders view your organization's performance.

Typical measures of this perspective involve market share, return on investment, cash flow, and cost reduction.

Customer perspective

The customer perspective takes into account the organization's customer service as well as its satisfaction ratings.

Measures relating to the customer perspective might include number of complaints, repeat purchases, delivery times, or returned items.

Process perspective

The aim of the process perspective is to identify how well a business is performing and to improve core competencies. This perspective also concerns other aspects such as manufacturing quality and employee motivation.

Process is usually measured in terms of efficiency improvements, increased productivity, and improvements in morale.

Learning and growth perspective

The goal of the learning and growth perspective is to improve and create value for the future of the organization. This takes into account aspects such as product development and diversification, as well as HR development.

This perspective is typically measured in terms of the number of new products introduced, amount of training provided, or number of employee suggestions.

Keep in mind that translating your strategy into a corporate balanced scorecard alone won't guarantee that employees will know how to execute it.

You still need to make a connection between your strategic objectives and employee tasks.

But you can overcome this gap in employee understanding by cascading your balanced scorecard.

Cascading balanced scorecards involves linking strategy to every level within your organization. As a leader, this means converting corporate-level strategy into different objectives for departments, teams, and individuals. This method aligns group tasks to strategic objectives, and ensures that organization-wide focus is consistent. It also enables information to flow from frontline staff up the organizational hierarchy. Relaying results and feedback about the strategy shows groups within your organization how their actions contribute to the strategy.

For example, suppose an airline company's strategy is to reduce its turnaround times. This strategy may be translated into increased training for the airline's Maintenance Department.

Different teams within the department could then be trained to repair airplanes by replacing parts rather than repairing them. Each engineer within a team could then keep a record of parts required to anticipate future problems, speeding up the maintenance process.

As it may be difficult to repair certain parts, replacing them with new parts could cut down on the amount of time spent servicing the airplanes, thereby reducing turnaround times. And by anticipating which parts may be required, engineers can reduce time spent locating the required parts, also helping to cut down on overall turnaround times.

Question

What is the purpose of cascading balanced scorecards?

Options:

1. Cascading allows senior managers to create an overarching corporate strategy that can be applied to any hierarchical level within an organization

2. Cascading is used to achieve alignment by translating overall strategy into objectives for business units, departments, and individuals

3. Cascading is a method of creating a set of fixed standards that can be used to evaluate employee performance throughout an organization

Answer

Option 1: This option is incorrect. A corporate strategy must first be converted into group- or individual- level objectives to be effective.

Option 2: This is the correct option. Cascading allows balanced scorecards to be developed at every level of an organization and links strategy to group or individual objectives.

Option 3: This option is incorrect. As different groups or individuals within an organization may have different objectives relating to an organizational strategy, creating fixed standards to assess employees may not be realistic.

Ensuring corporate BSC is understood

Your organization's corporate strategy is represented by a high-level balanced scorecard. But to execute this strategy, you need to translate this high-level scorecard into department, team, and individual scorecards. Once the different unit scorecards have been created, supervisors and team leaders must decide what the tasks are that align with team, departmental, and corporate objectives. By linking personal tasks to goals outlined in the financial, customer, process, or learning and growth perspectives, employees are more likely to support your strategy.

There are three key principles for cascading balanced scorecards:
- you have to ensure that the high-level scorecard is clearly understood,
- each business unit must select the objective it can execute, ensuring that its scorecard links back to the high-level scorecard, and

- all the business unit scorecards combined must cover all of the high-level objectives.

The first principle of cascading BSCs is to ensure the high-level scorecard is clearly understood. Because corporate balanced scorecards identify key measures of success, it's essential that everyone understands these measures and related objectives before creating their own scorecards. This is especially true of individuals responsible for developing scorecards within departments and teams. If these individuals don't fully understand the corporate objectives and measures, they may find it difficult to construct scorecards that are truly aligned to corporate goals.

For example, suppose a company's high-level scorecard states that its strategy is to increase customer loyalty.

Without a deep understanding of this strategy, leaders may not be able to translate the corporate scorecard into objectives for employees working in different departments and teams.

However, if senior management communicates the high-level scorecard effectively, leaders can define departmental objectives, such as measuring customer value or profiling ideal customers.

Reflect

What do you think are the most effective ways of communicating your organization's corporate scorecard?

Write down your response or enter it in a text file in your word-processor application (or in a text editor such as Notepad) and save it to your hard drive for later viewing.

You may have noted that you can ensure your high-level scorecard is understood by creating extensive communication and education programs. Or you could disseminate your corporate scorecard using a local intranet, or with presentations, newsletters, and brochures.

Keep in mind that the best method of communicating your scorecard is to use face-to-face sessions. Make sure you involve the people who have to develop scorecards with business units, such as team leaders, supervisors, or line managers.

These sessions can take the form of one-to-one or group meetings, and can provide leaders with the opportunity to review each measure or objective. They can discuss the significance of the scorecard for their units, and develop specific strategies for ensuring their scorecards align with the corporate scorecard.

Take Andrew, for example. He's a chief communications officer at Phlogistix, a multinational pharmaceutical company. His company's sales figures have been declining over the last year, and senior management has devised a new strategy of broadening its range of products. Andrew's team is responsible for creating the corporate scorecard and cascading it to departments and other business units.

Andrew first considers the financial perspective and makes increasing revenue its main objective. The customer objective is to launch better value generic medication, while the internal process objective is to identify and target new partners. Finally, the objective of the learning and growth perspective is to develop internal marketing and commercial skills.

Andrew then includes this scorecard in a company-wide newsletter. He also organizes several group sessions with the heads of the Sales, Manufacturing, and R&D

Departments to discuss these objectives and their implications for team goals.

Choosing objectives that can be executed

The next principle of cascading BSCs is that each business unit should examine the high-level scorecard and select the objective that it can execute. When choosing objectives, departments should first consider each perspective. There may be several objectives within each perspective, so each department must examine its functions, values, or skills to identify an objective it can influence.

For instance, suppose a manufacturing company's corporate BSC has a financial objective of improving overall efficiency. A business unit such as the Shipping Department may decide that it can influence this goal and adopt it as its own objective. It can then choose a different method of measuring the objective, such as a reduction in shipping fees.

Teams within the Shipping Department could also adopt this objective but use different ways of measuring their success. For example, one team could negotiate fees with suppliers to reduce spending. A different team could find ways of reducing packaging materials.

The objectives of both these teams are linked to the Shipping Department's objective. This objective is in turn aligned with the corporate scorecard. Keep in mind that the aim of cascading BSCs is to ensure that every business-unit-level scorecard created links back to the high-level scorecard. The objectives and measures outlined in high-level or corporate scorecards should influence all subsequent BSCs developed down the organizational hierarchy.

Question

When choosing objectives from the high-level scorecard, each department should select an objective from each of the four scorecard perspectives.

Is this statement true or false?

Options:

1. True
2. False

Answer

Option 1: This statement is not true. The objectives detailed in each of the corporate scorecard perspectives may not apply to the particular functions or abilities of a team or department. Departments should only pick the objectives they believe they can execute.

Option 2: This statement is false. Departments should only choose objectives that they think they can influence. They're not obliged to choose one from each of the four perspectives in the corporate scorecard.

Consider the corporate scorecard of Phlogistix. Having reviewed the corporate scorecard, the R&D Department considers the customer perspective's aim of launching better value medication. Employees in the R&D Department believe they can have a major impact on this objective, and carry it forward to their own scorecard.

However, they change the method for measuring this objective to something they feel will narrow the scope of actions – increasing their output of generic medications by 50%. They believe generic medication offers a cheaper alternative to branded products, which will appeal to customers.

The R&D Department comprises different groups, one of which is the R&D operations group. This group is responsible for implementing studies into new products. Employees within this group who report to the R&D Department start reviewing its scorecard. Operations staff members decide that by increasing the percentage of studies related to generic products by 30%, they can successfully impact the objective of the R&D Department.

Covering all high-level objectives

The final principle when cascading BSCs is that all the business unit scorecards combined should cover all the high-level objectives. Just because your organization has created scorecards for each department, unit, or team doesn't necessarily mean they're all aligned to the high-level objectives.

Once each level of cascading has been completed, you need to examine the scorecards created to make sure they align with the corporate scorecard. Each team or department needs to evaluate its scorecard to ensure there's a visible correlation between that scorecard and the high-level one.

Once this evaluation is finished, teams in higher levels could meet with scorecard developers in lower levels to give advice on how they may improve their scorecards. You could also provide teams from different business units the opportunity to review each others' scorecards. Collaboration between these diverse groups allows for greater objective input and transparency within your organization.

But what if all your high-level objectives have not been covered by these cascaded scorecards? Sometimes your corporate-level objectives may be unrealistic. That's why you must review their validity. Poorly defined or unachievable objectives may lead to misallocated resources or frustrated employees.

Consider the pharmaceutical company Phlogistix again. As the company's corporate scorecard is cascaded to each level, employees check that their objectives align with the high-level scorecard and actually contribute to the company's strategy.

The company also shares and circulates scorecards from different departments. Having noted that the R&D Department is going to start increasing its output of generic medications, the Sales Department decides to collaborate with the operations group to refine its own scorecard.

Question

What practices should you follow when cascading your corporate balanced scorecard?

Options:

1. Each single team or department within your organization should cover all the objectives outlined in the corporate scorecard

2. Get different departments and teams within your organization to choose objectives that align with the high-level scorecard

3. Ensure that all the corporate scorecard's objectives are covered by the department, team, and individual scorecards combined

4. Make sure that all levels within your organization understand the corporate scorecard

5. Ensure that each department creates a scorecard that supports its own goals and objectives

Answer

Option 1: This option is incorrect. Each unit within your organization should only pick the objectives that it thinks it can have an influence on.

Option 2: This option is correct. It's crucial that each business unit selects an objective that corresponds to the high-level scorecard so that it's implemented effectively.

Option 3: This option is correct. If the corporate scorecard has been cascaded effectively, business unit and individual scorecards combined should comprise all the high-level objectives.

Option 4: This option is correct. Each business unit in your organization must be able to understand the high-level scorecard so that it can select an objective it can influence and choose its own measures.

Option 5: This option is incorrect. Each department, team, or individual scorecard should link to and support the high-level scorecard objectives.

Learning aid - Cascading High-level Scorecards
Your organization's corporate strategy is represented by a high-level scorecard. To execute this strategy, you need to translate this corporate scorecard into departmental, team, and individual scorecards by following three important principles.

Principles	Methods
Ensure high-level scorecard is understood because it contains the objectives and measures that inform everyone of the strategic theme	Develop an extensive communication or education program, or disseminate your corporate scorecard using a local intranet, presentations, newsletters, or brochures. Use one-to-one or group meetings to provide leaders with the opportunity to review each measure or objective outlined in the scorecard.
Each business unit should select the objective it can execute, ensuring that its scorecard links back to the high-level scorecard	Each department should first consider the objectives outlined in the financial, customer, process, and learning and growth perspectives. It must then examine its own functions, values, or skills to identify an objective it can influence.
All the business unit scorecards combined should cover all of the high-level objectives	Each team or department needs to evaluate its scorecards to ensure there's a visible correlation between its scorecard and the high-level one. Once this evaluation is finished, teams in higher levels could meet with scorecard developers in lower levels to give advice on how they may improve their scorecards. You could also provide teams from different business units with the opportunity to review each other's scorecards. If all high-level objectives haven't been covered by the cascaded scorecards, you must review the validity of these objectives.

Personal and strategic objectives

When cascading your corporate scorecard, you must link employees' personal objectives with your organization's strategy. Once you've aligned individual scorecards to the high-level scorecard, you need to create a clear picture for your staff of how their tasks can affect the success of the strategy.

Bear in mind three key guidelines when linking personal and strategic objectives. First, ensure the right people are in place to execute the strategy. Tie incentives to strategic objectives and measures. And support employees' personal objectives with an action plan.

The first guideline when linking personal and strategic objectives is to ensure the right people are in place. As a leader, you must evaluate employees fairly to make sure you have the right mix of skills, personalities, and attitudes to move your strategy forward. When assessing employees, you need to know what abilities are required to implement each strategic position. But you must also be prepared to make the tough decisions about the people who don't have the right skills.

Know abilities required

Certain skills and abilities may be critical to the successful implementation of your strategy. But without accurate knowledge and appraisal of each role, people without the requisite skills may end up slowing the process down.

When evaluating each role, outline the criteria that are essential to that particular position. For example, do your line managers or supervisors have the communication skills required to turn your strategy into actions? Or do your frontline staff members have sufficient training to carry out their tasks adequately?

Make tough decisions

Once you've evaluated each role, you'll have to deal with the nonperformers – the people who aren't performing up to the standards required of their positions.

A strong leader doesn't hesitate to make changes to ensure the business strategy is executed effectively. These changes can include replacing employees or moving them to a more suitable position.

The next guideline to keep in mind is to tie incentives to strategic objectives and measures. Linking incentives to individual scorecards can be an effective way of motivating your employees to execute your strategy.

Supervisors can help employees validate their personal objectives by encouraging them to develop their own scorecards.

In some organizations, employees set their own targets – for example, to reduce costs, improve work processes, or increase their product knowledge.

Another way of supporting employees to follow through with their scorecards is to link incentive compensation to their own scorecard measures.

By linking incentives to your employees' own performance measures, your organization can demonstrate that it's serious about each individual's strategic objective. It also shows that your organization isn't just focused on short-term goals, but also on enhancing employees' skills for the long-term benefit of the company.

Bear in mind that while individual awards can motivate employees to improve their performance, such awards might also impair teamwork and knowledge sharing. One way of avoiding this may be to devise awards based on overall departmental performance.

The final guideline when linking personal and strategic objectives is to support personal objectives with an action plan. Employees are more likely to execute your organization's strategy if they can follow a well-defined set of steps. Before creating an action plan, you need to ask who'll actually develop the plan, and find out who's responsible for its implementation. What are the action steps? Who's accountable for each step? And what resources are required?

Seet each question relating to creating an action plan for more information.

Who'll develop plan?

When first deciding on an action plan, the importance of those who put the plan together is often overlooked.

In most cases, the team that will execute the plan is instrumental in its development. This is because that team has a vested interest in ensuring the plan is executed successfully.

Who's responsible for implementation?

In order to monitor and evaluate the action plan, the team will need to assign someone to review the plan and report on its progress.

This person, usually the team manager, must communicate any setbacks or problems the team is encountering in executing the plan. This person should explain what help or resources the team requires.

What are the steps?

The action plan should include a list of clear and concise steps. These should be written down in chronological order to avoid confusion and so that all team members involved can agree on what's required of them.

Who's accountable for each step?

While creating an action plan, the team leader needs to translate each step in the plan into specific tasks. These tasks should then be assigned to different individuals within the team. The team members will then take responsibility for the particular step in the action plan they're involved in.

What resources are required?

In order to accomplish each step in the action plan, the team leader has to identify resources needed by the team. These resources include financial, equipment, and human resources.

Remember the R&D Department at Phlogistix? The head of this department first carries out a review of the requirements of the operations managers. As his department will be expanding its production of generic medications, he decides these managers must complete an intensive training course. This is to ensure they have the knowledge to deal with regulatory compliance issues.

He then plans an incentives program whereby employees will be awarded company shares once the department reaches it target output.

The operations manager also develops a plan to make sure frontline staff members can handle the new production process. In the plan, she outlines specific projects to be accomplished and how employees' tasks will be monitored, and details any new equipment required by her team.

Question

Which examples demonstrate effective ways of helping employees link personal goals with strategic objectives?

Options:

1. Mei enrolls her employees in an online training course to make sure they know how to use new customer management software

2. Robin tries to motivate his employees by moving nonperformers in his team to another department in order to improve his company's sales figures

3. To expand his company's global presence, Omar outlines a plan in which members of his team are responsible for analyzing different key market targets

4. Bhadrak gives his employees the opportunity to change his company's strategic objectives to suit their abilities

5. Karen awards her team members with a 5% salary bonus after they meet their sales target for the quarter

Answer

Option 1: This option is correct. Employees must have the right skills and capabilities to implement an organization's strategy.

Option 2: This option is incorrect. To motivate employees, it's better to correlate incentives with objectives and measures outlined in their scorecards.

Option 3: This option is correct. By developing an action plan, employees will have a better idea of what their tasks and responsibilities are, and will see how these relate to the organization's strategy.

Option 4: This option is incorrect. Rather than changing company strategy to correspond to employee capabilities, it's better to have the right employees in place to carry out the tasks required of the strategy.

Option 5: This option is correct. Tying incentives to performance is an effective method of motivating employees to achieve strategic objectives.

Recognizing competencies

As a leader, you must nurture a talented workforce to help your organization execute its strategy. Decisions about strategic direction are essentially decisions about talent. So having the right people with the right competencies is vital to turning your organization's vision into a reality. But how can you promote these desired competencies among your employees? One way is to examine your overall strategy, as well as employees' objectives in achieving it, and find out if they have the required skill set.

Organizations are increasingly reliant on having people with the right competencies. To achieve strategic goals such as improving services, reducing costs, or becoming more innovative, organizations require employees with specific skill sets. Creating an executable strategy means having the desired competency in place. This can either be achieved at the selection stage or by training employees as needed. And as some skill sets may become obsolete due to changing market trends, leaders must modify competencies by upskilling employees to meet new demands.

Understanding competencies is critical to identifying qualities needed to execute a strategic objective. But what exactly are competencies? Competencies are any useful behaviors, technical skills, attitudes, or abilities that can produce a positive result.

Competencies focus on an employee's unique characteristics, rather than on tasks or responsibilities that could also apply to other members of staff.

And as competencies take into account the skills and abilities required in a particular role, they provide a good basis for measuring employee performance.

The three main types of competencies that you should bear in mind are knowledge, skills, and values.

See each type of competency for more information.

Knowledge

Knowledge refers to an employee's education or level of expertise in a particular area. For some positions, employees may need to have specific product knowledge or a deep understanding of key market targets.

Skill

Skills relate to the way employees apply their knowledge. For example, this might concern how well employees operate certain equipment, manage their time, collaborate with other employees, plan meetings, or deal with customers.

Other important abilities are leadership, interpersonal, and problem-solving skills.

Values

Values refer to the mindset or personality traits that help employees perform the tasks required of your strategy. Some key employee values are customer focus, innovation, creativity, motivation, and goal orientation.

Other important employee values include flexibility, professionalism, honesty, and loyalty.

While employee knowledge and skills can be developed using education or communication programs, it can be difficult to instill the right values in employees.

This is something that usually involves careful selection by HR managers. They need to look for employees with the appropriate values during the hiring process.

If your employees don't have the right values, your organization may need to review its HR strategy to ensure future objectives can be implemented more effectively. But remember that certain values can be promoted through the use of effective incentive schemes.

Question

Match each type of competency to the corresponding description.

Options:

A. Knowledge

B. Skills

C. Values

Targets:

1. A person's education or level of expertise in a particular area

2. The ability to operate certain equipment, manage time, or collaborate with employees

3. A mindset or specific personality traits such as customer focus, innovation, or loyalty

Answer

Knowledge relates to an employee's understanding or experience in a specific professional area.

Skills can refer to the application of knowledge in a given situation, such as handling a phone call professionally or performing an audit.

Values involve the principles that people bring to their tasks and that drive their behavior and commitment.

Five steps to assess employee competency

Clearly, competent employees are one of your organization's most valuable resources. Without the right knowledge, skills, and values in place, it can be a costly and time-wasting exercise to implement your organization's strategy. So how do you know if employees have the strategic competencies that can turn your plan into a reality? And what can you do if they lack certain crucial skills? One way to address this is by assessing employees' competencies and measuring gaps in their knowledge and skills.

You should keep five key steps in mind when measuring competency gaps. First create a list of competencies required for each position. Second, assess your employees' existing competencies using different assessment methods. Third, identify gaps in an employee's portfolio of competencies. The next step is to create a development plan to address the existing gaps.

And finally, monitor your development plan and evaluate its progress.

Assessing employee competencies enables you to find out whether employees have the right knowledge, skills, and values to implement your organization's strategy.

It allows you to define the performance expectations of a particular role, as well as its minimum requirements.

And by evaluating the competencies of your workforce, you can help to cultivate employees' talent and abilities for your organization's future benefit.

Question

Put the five steps of the competency assessment process in the correct order.

Options:

A. Create list of competencies

B. Assess employees' existing competencies

C. Identify gaps in portfolio of competencies

D. Create plan to address gaps

E. Monitor plan and evaluate progress

Answer

Correct answer(s):

Create list of competencies is ranked the first step. You first have to define the requirements of the strategic position by creating a list of competencies.

Assess employees' existing competencies is ranked the second step. The second step is to evaluate what knowledge, skills, and values employees currently have.

Identify gaps in portfolio of competencies is ranked the third step. The third step is to analyze what employees' weaknesses are.

Create plan to address gaps is ranked the fourth step. The fourth step involves developing a plan to improve critical employee skills or expertise.

Monitor plan and evaluate progress is ranked the fifth step. The final step is to review your employees' progress with their development plans.

Listing and assessing competencies

The first step in assessing employee competencies is to create a detailed list of competencies required for each strategic position in your organization.

Before listing the requirements of each target job, consider the factors that may affect the position. These can include changes in company structure, new industry standards and marketplace trends, or changes in technology.

For each job, you could then examine the related requirements. What tasks are necessary for its completion? What are the performance outcome measures? And what skills are required to complete the job effectively?

For instance, suppose you're assessing a software programming position. You might first examine if there have been any recent developments in the software industry, such as new design methodologies, that employees should be aware of.

You could review the position's performance expectations, such as the ability to work in a fast-paced environment and handle multiple tasks simultaneously.

You could also consider what qualifications employees should have. And you might assess which programming languages are essential, or desired, for the particular position.

Take Samuel, for example. He's an HR manager at a large accounting firm. His company is planning to expand its range of services by acquiring one of its main competitors. It's Samuel's responsibility to identify employee competency gaps that may impair the successful execution of this strategy.

Samuel first looks into some of the key competencies required of supervisors in his company. He knows that the supervisors will play a central role in guiding and monitoring teams comprising employees from both companies.

Having analyzed the supervisor's role, he outlines a number of core competencies. A supervisor has to be able to gain acceptance as a leader, deal with performance problems, and manage conflicts between employees.

The second step to keep in mind is to assess your employees' existing competencies. Once you've created a list of job-specific requirements, you can use various methods to evaluate how well your employees' capabilities match up to these requirements. Three common methods are self-assessments, manager assessments, and 360-degree assessments.

See each assessment method for more information.

Self-assessments

The purpose of the self-assessment is to allow employees to evaluate themselves against a list of different competencies, behaviors, and outputs. Each behavior can be rated along a sliding scale from, for example, excellent to poor.

There are several benefits of using this type of assessment: it allows individuals to reflect on their own strengths and weaknesses, it's quick to fill out, and it can be processed easily once all the data has been entered. A disadvantage, however, is that it's subjective and, as a result, may not be completely accurate.

There are a number of different competencies included in the self-assessment, and each competency area includes several related questions. The self-assessment asks employees to review each competency area included in the assessment and to rate themselves on a scale of 1 to 4, where 4 is outstanding and 1 is unsatisfactory.

Manager assessments

A manager assessment evaluates how a manager's direct reports match the competency requirements for a specific job. Managers complete the assessment based on how well they think their reports perform the behaviors linked to the competencies.

Like the employee self-assessment, the manager assessment can be completed and processed quickly. However, this assessment only provides one point of view. It may not take into account other employee assets such as an ability to get along with teammates or an employee's customer focus.

There are a number of different competencies included in the manager assessment, and each competency area includes several related questions. The manager assessment asks managers to review each competency area included in the assessment and to rate their employees on a scale of 1 to 4, where 4 is outstanding and 1 is unsatisfactory.

360-degree assessments

The 360-degree assessment is a comprehensive evaluation that includes information from managers, peers, and customers, as well as the individual employees being assessed.

This approach provides a more objective assessment of an employee's competencies. And by seeing how their self assessments compare to assessments from their peers and managers, employees may be motivated to improve their performance. One disadvantage is that some groups, such as customers, may not be able to make a fair assessment of an employee's competencies as they can't observe the individual's full range of behaviors.

Having listed the essential competencies for the position of technical support supervisor, Samuel, the HR manager at the accounting firm, develops an employee self-assessment form. In this form, he first gets employees to assess how well they think they can gain acceptance as supervisors from their reports.

The assessment also asks employees about their ability to deal with performance problems. Finally, employees are asked to rate how well they manage conflict in the workplace.

Analyzing gaps in competencies

The next step in the competency assessment process is to identify gaps in an employee's portfolio of competencies. At this stage, you need to compare the results of your employee assessment to the requirements of the position. This helps to clarify the difference between what employees are doing and what they should be doing.

A competency assessment can often highlight your employees' strengths and weaknesses. It may reveal the areas individuals need to work on in order to reach a required output or a standard level of customer service.

For instance, some employees may have a lot of expertise in a particular area but lack the ability to communicate their knowledge to their teammates. Other employees, on the other hand, may have the right skills but lack the motivation or customer focus to further your organization's strategy.

Bear in mind that whatever weaknesses have been highlighted, you need to prioritize the competency that has been rated lowest in the self-, manager, or 360-degree assessments.

Consider Samuel again. He's processed the data from the employee self-assessments, and has set the desired level of competence for each requirement.

He then compares this to the actual results of the employee self-assessment. Using this data, Samuel is able to identify that the ability to handle conflict is the biggest gap in the supervisors' portfolio of competencies.

Question

Match each example to the step in the competency assessment process that it corresponds to.

Options:

A. Michael outlines six key capabilities that fashion retail assistants in his department must demonstrate to help boost his company's sales figures

B. Ayana gets clients, colleagues, and managers to evaluate some of the software designers working in her department

C. Rashaundra notes that some of her employees in the Marketing Department have lots of expertise in advertising but haven't gained any new client contracts

Targets:

1. Create list of competencies
2. Assess employees' existing competencies
3. Identify gaps in portfolio of competencies

Answer

By creating a list of the key competencies of fashion retail assistants, Michael has carried out the first step in identifying employee performance gaps.

Ayana uses the 360-degree assessment method to evaluate her employees' existing expertise and skills.

Rashaundra identifies that her employees' customer focus competency isn't as strong as the role requires it to be.

Creating and monitoring plans

The next step in the process of assessing employee competency is to create a development plan to address gaps in your employees' portfolios of competencies. Once you know what your employees' weaknesses are, you'll have a better idea of how to ensure they have the right knowledge, skills, or values to execute your strategy. Each individual's development plan should provide specific details about the person's learning goals and how to achieve them.

When creating a development plan, there are a number of guidelines to keep in mind. First, provide the employee's name, as well as the person who the employee should report to, such as a supervisor. Outline competency areas to be addressed, as well as learning objectives for each competency. Describe the actions to be taken to accomplish each objective. Detail any resources needed. And provide a time frame by outlining the plan's start and completion dates.

The final step is to monitor your development plan and evaluate its progress. There are number of questions you need to ask to ensure your plan is being implemented effectively. For example, are employees actually learning the skills required for the position. And have all assignments and courses been completed satisfactorily? During this stage, supervisors could also create a survey asking employees to evaluate their development plan. They should also debrief the employees to determine if their expectations were met.

Remember Samuel? He decides to tackle key gaps in his employees' competencies by enrolling them in an online conflict management course. He also gets supervisors to complete a two-day in-house seminar about conflict resolution in the workplace.

The supervisors then report to the project manager, who verifies that they've finished the course and completed any related tests.

Finally, the supervisors give feedback about the course and seminar, highlighting how appropriate the training was for their current positions and responsibilities.

Case Study: Question 1 of 2
Scenario

Leonard is a senior sales manager at a major food distribution company. His company is planning to introduce some of its existing products into new markets to increase sales. Leonard must ensure the Sales Department employees have the right competencies to execute this strategy.

Leonard first examines the sales representative position and outlines three vital requirements – the ability to generate new leads, work well as part of a team, and have strong presentation skills.

He then devises an assessment form for the company's regional managers, which they use to evaluate individuals in their sales teams. Having analyzed the resulting data, Leonard finds that many representatives have poor presentation skills. He decides to get sales employees to complete an online presentation skills course. After a number of weeks, Leonard discovers that some employees haven't started the course yet, while others found the course wasn't relevant to what they wanted to learn.

Examine how Leonard develops his employees' competencies and answer the questions in order.

Question

In what ways does Leonard develop his employees' competencies effectively?

Options:

1. He creates a list of competencies required for the sales representative position

2. He uses a comprehensive method to evaluate his employees' competencies

3. He pinpoints an area where the sales representatives' skills are lacking

4. He follows up closely to review how employees are progressing with their development plans

5. He comes up with an effective plan to address gaps in employee skills

Answer

Option 1: This option is correct. It's essential to first outline what competencies are needed for the strategic position so that gaps in relevant skills or knowledge can then be identified.

Option 2: This option is incorrect. Leonard uses a manager assessment, which only provides one point of view when evaluating employees.

Option 3: This option is correct. Leonard uses a manager assessment form to identify presentation skills as a key competency that his employees are missing.

Option 4: This option is incorrect. Leonard only finds out several weeks after introducing the development plan that employees aren't adhering to their plans.

Option 5: This option is correct. Leonard arranges for employees to take an online course that's aimed specifically at improving presentation skills.

Case Study: Question 2 of 2

Scenario

Leonard is a senior sales manager at a major food distribution company. His company is planning to introduce some of its existing products into new markets to increase sales. Leonard must ensure the Sales Department employees have the right competencies to execute this strategy.

Leonard first examines the sales representative position and outlines three vital requirements – the ability to generate new leads, work well as part of a team, and have strong presentation skills.

He then devises an assessment form for the company's regional managers, which they use to evaluate individuals in their sales teams. Having analyzed the resulting data, Leonard finds that many representatives have poor presentation skills. He decides to get sales employees to complete an online presentation skills course. After a number of weeks, Leonard discovers that some employees haven't started the course yet, while others found the course wasn't relevant to what they wanted to learn.

Examine how Leonard develops his employees' competencies and answer the questions in order.

Question

How could Leonard have developed his employees' competencies more effectively?

Options:

1. He should have gotten employees to create their own development plans

2. He should have asked supervisors to monitor the sales representatives' plans

3. He should have created a development plan for each of the competencies required for the position

4. He should have used a number of different assessment methods

Answer

Option 1: This option is incorrect. It's the responsibility of the manager or supervisor to create a development plan for employees.

Option 2: This is the correct option. To ensure that employees are learning the skills needed for the position, it's vital for supervisors or managers to monitor their employees' progress closely.

Option 3: This option is incorrect. When devising development plans, managers should prioritize employees' weakest competencies.

Option 4: This option is correct. As one of the required competencies of the position was to work well as part of a team, Leonard might have included a peer assessment to ensure he was evaluating his employees accurately.

Activity - **Assessing Employee Competencies**

You can print this document, or recreate the table in a word processing or spreadsheet application, and use it to complete this activity.

To ensure your organization's strategy is implemented effectively, you need to make sure you have the right people in the right places. Analyzing employee competencies and job requirements is one way of finding out how to develop your employees' skills for the benefit of your organization.

Steps

1. List the competencies required for the position

2. List competencies that the typical employee currently possesses

3. Identify gaps between the competencies required in the job and the employees' existing competencies

4. Note the elements – the competency areas and learning objectives – that should be included in the employees' development plans

CHAPTER FOUR

Monitoring and Evaluating Initiatives

Balanced scorecards and action plans

Organizations spend a lot of time and resources on developing effective business strategies. However, strategies are only useful when they're implemented effectively. To ensure that the company's plan is carried out and aligns with current business needs, strategy execution needs to be monitored on an ongoing basis.

Reflect

Think about your own experience of bringing initiatives to completion. Why do you think it's important to monitor execution of strategy?

Write down your response or enter it in a text file in your word-processor application (or in a text editor such as Notepad) and save it to your hard drive for later viewing and for comparison with the alternate opinion that follows.

Importance of monitoring strategy

As you may have noted, monitoring provides a link between the written plan and day-to-day operations, ensuring you stay on track and that results align with strategic objectives. It allows for corrective action and fine tuning or changing strategy in the face of changes or problems with plans. Monitoring also improves performance by achieving buy-in and ensuring accountability.

Monitoring can be a complex process. You can use four methods to keep track of completion of strategic goals, including balanced scorecards and action plans, strategic dashboards, strategic review meetings, and employee engagement reviews.

The balanced scorecard, used prodigiously in business, measures the organization's activities in terms of its strategies. It gives managers a comprehensive view of the company's performance. The scorecard translates the organization's strategy into four perspectives: financial, customer, learning and growth, and business processes.

Scorecards start with strategy maps, made up of smaller objectives that feed into the overall corporate goals. In order to achieve the organizational goals, different business units will have different objectives or responsibilities. Through a process known as cascading of the strategy map, each department in the organization creates its own strategy map. This ultimately links every employee's goals and performance with the top-level organizational scorecard.

Successful companies implement their strategic plans by translating departmental strategy maps into action plans for each employee. The first method of monitoring is action plans. Action plans prevent confusion or complacency about what has to be done. They divide strategic aims into solid, clearly-defined steps.

Action plan steps include clearly defined work assignments, each of which are assigned to a specific employee and must be completed within a specified period of time.

Then an organizational action plan is drawn up. It lists each intended action plan step and work assignment in chronological order. This helps the organization to decide when and where resources will need to be assigned for each department. It also makes specific people accountable for the implementation of each step and the delivery of each assignment. The progress of each step should be monitored regularly and assignments followed up on.

Question

A company has a strategic objective to improve customer satisfaction rates by 25% by the end of the year.

What steps can it take to monitor the implementation of this goal as part of an action plan?

Options:

1. Generate a strategy map that is cascaded down through each relevant department

2. Have each department break down the strategic goal into action steps and work assignments

3. Assign names and due dates to the delivery and implementation of each necessary step

4. Have all departments focus on the same strategic objectives

5. Let each department relevant to the goal set its own deadlines

Answer

Option 1: This option is correct. The high-level goal can be translated into smaller goals for each department contributing toward its achievement.

Option 2: This option is correct. Strategic goals are achieved when they are broken down into individual action steps as part of an action plan.

Option 3: This option is correct. In addition to breaking down goals into action steps, a department must set dates and responsibilities for the delivery of tasks.

Option 4: This option is incorrect. A strategy map should be generated for each relevant department.

Option 5: This option is incorrect. Each department develops its own action plan but this is incorporated into the overall organizational action plan and monitored at corporate level.

Strategic dashboards

Executives at the corporate level can integrate and monitor scorecard perspectives using a second method of monitoring – strategic dashboards. These dashboards help to link management reporting to the execution of strategic objectives. Sometimes the term "dashboard" is confused with the concept of scorecards. However, strategic dashboards contain much more information than scorecards. Scorecards act merely as a snapshot of the organization's performance or key performance indicators (KPIs) against certain business targets at any given point in time.

Strategic dashboards provide the same information as scorecards but include detailed feedback. This feedback can include reports, statistical data, analyses, or graphs. Those using the dashboard can typically view the data in several different formats, share it with others, and print it.

In large organizations, department heads may have strategic dashboards relevant to their own action plans.

However, this type of information is probably most relevant at the executive level, as it groups related scorecards and report views to provide an overall picture of strategic progress.

There are a number of key benefits to using strategic dashboards for tracking strategic objectives: it allows for top-down tracking at executive level it's a powerful way to combine multiple views into a single display management can quickly assess the "health" of the company, and it enables management to quickly respond to business issues

See each benefit of using strategic dashboards for more information.

Top-down tracking

Executives can view the information gathered from each business unit and department in the organization in one place. It provides a high-level overview of strategic progress that top-level management can drill down into.

Single display

Feedback from the implementation of strategic objectives can be viewed from multiple angles. Strategic dashboards allow you to combine these multiple views into a single display for convenience and efficiency.

Quickly assess "health"

A high-level, single-view feature means that executives can use strategic dashboards to quickly assess the current status or "health" of the organization at any given point in time. It displays standardized accurate information in the form of charts, key performance indicators – KPIs – and other relevant feedback methods.

Quickly respond

Because management can quickly assess the current status of strategic objectives, it can respond quickly if a problem arises.

For example, if a KPI is particularly low or an objective is showing no sign of success, executives might decide to respond by reviewing and changing the current strategy map and action plans.

Question

An electronics company plans to launch a new device in the coming months. One of its strategic objectives is to acquire 15% market share in this product category within 12 months of launch.

Which examples represent ways that executives can monitor the implementation of this objective using strategic dashboards?

Options:

1. The VP of Marketing checks the progress of the product development team each week and compares results to the product release schedule

2. The CEO uses the dashboard to compare feedback results from all departments involved in the new device project

3. The heads of Finance and Marketing use the dashboard after launch to assess the current market share acquired by the new product each week

4. Executives use the strategic dashboard for KPIs and other performance indicators on progress but use scorecards for more detailed feedback reports

5. Workers on the factory floor use the dashboard to check how they are performing compared to their colleagues

Answer

Option 1: This option is correct. Strategic dashboards allow executives to quickly assess the status of strategic objectives.

Option 2: This option is correct. Multiple views of feedback can be combined into a single display on the dashboard so you can monitor objectives at a high level.

Option 3: This option is correct. The dashboard allows a quick assessment of the "health" of the organization and its performance on certain KPIs.

Option 4: This option is incorrect. Scorecards only provide KPIs and other performance indicators, but dashboards provide much more detailed feedback in addition to this.

Option 5: This option is incorrect. Strategic dashboards are used as a high-level, top-down monitoring tool, usually by department heads or corporate executives.

Strategic review meetings

A key use of strategic dashboards is to provide information during quarterly strategy review meetings. Review meetings are the third method you can use to monitor implementation. The purpose of strategy review meetings is to discuss the progress of the organizational strategy map by tracking the scorecards of each department. Attendees propose ways to improve performance and achieve goals.

The meetings aren't used to alter strategy, but to solve any progress problems that have emerged after examining the data. Department heads complete their scorecards using recent reports, trends, and KPI data from the dashboard.

The scorecards are circulated so that executives can review feedback and drill down further if necessary using the dashboard. All attendees must come to strategy review meetings fully prepared and aware of relevant issues and problems. Executives can then steer the meeting appropriately based on the scorecards provided.

The meetings aren't designed for attendees to listen passively to reports. Instead, strategy reviews are used for active discussion.

During the discussion, attendees check that strategy execution is on track. They identify risks together, highlight implementation problems, and discuss why the problems are occurring. Finally, and most important, they decide what corrective actions need to be taken. Responsibility for the implementation of these actions is then assigned to the appropriate people.

Question

An energy company is approaching the end of the first quarter since its new strategy map was launched. One of the strategic goals is to explore new markets for expansion and diversification.

Which steps should the company's executives take to prepare for the review of this strategy?

Options:

1. The head of the Research and Development Department prepares and circulates a scorecard summarizing the department's progress in researching new products

2. The chairperson of the strategy review meeting sets an agenda that will focus primarily on the Marketing Department's current problems with breaking new markets

3. A number of corrective actions are agreed upon at the meeting and responsibility for implementing those actions is given to the Marketing and Finance VPs

4. Attendees at the meeting listen to a series of long reports from each department before discussion begins

5. Attendees are invited to the meeting to present their suggestions for changing the overall strategic goals

Answer

Option 1: This option is correct. Department heads prepare scorecards using KPIs and performance results to inform executives before strategy review meetings.

Option 2: This option is correct. Information circulated before the meeting helps executives to steer the meeting so that important problems can be discussed.

Option 3: This option is correct. An important function of strategy review meetings is to determine which actions are needed going forward and who will be responsible for implementing them.

Option 4: This option is incorrect. Strategy review meetings are designed for active discussion. Detailed information is circulated before the meeting begins.

Option 5: This option is incorrect. Strategy review meetings aren't about changing strategy. They're about reviewing progress being made toward current goals.

Reviewing employee engagement

Reviewing employee engagement is the fourth method for monitoring implementation. This is a key metric, as engaged employees can increase profitability and customer loyalty. Organizations may neglect this metric during difficult times, but engaged employees always play a key role in implementing an organization's strategy. Therefore, you should try to ensure, through monitoring, that engagement levels are kept in check.

Engagement differs from satisfaction or motivation. It can be difficult to measure and elusive to define. Every organization creates and measures engagement in its own way.

The way in which engagement is defined and measured can change as circumstances inside or outside the organization change. Executives should take an "engagement temperature" at least once a year to monitor any changes.

Corrective actions are then implemented to rectify any drops in engagement. If engagement is low, strategic objectives will suffer.

There are three key steps involved in reviewing employee engagement. First, you should measure engagement by using methods such as surveys, interviews, and focus groups that are tailored to the organizational strategy. You should then use the results to take necessary action. Finally, you should ensure these reviews are conducted annually.

See each of the key steps involved in reviewing employee engagement to learn why each one is important.

1. Measure

Each organization needs to decide on the best way to assess engagement in its workforce. This will depend on the operations of that company.

For example, interviews with each employee may be appropriate for one company but surveys or focus groups might be more practical for a very large workforce.

2. Take action on results

Once you have asked employees for feedback, you must act on the results. If you conduct surveys and focus groups, for example, employees may become less engaged if they feel their opinions aren't listened to.

3. Review annually

To ensure that the engagement is continuously aligned with strategic objectives, it should be reviewed annually. Engagement levels may change at different times for different reasons. If employees are to be kept engaged and contribute toward strategy implementation, they should be assessed regularly.

Question

Business Execution

A large retail company has been rolling out a new customer service strategy for the last year. Executives want to ensure that the objectives are implemented correctly.

Which steps might they take to effectively review employee engagement?

Options:

1. A full-scale assessment of employee engagement levels is implemented using employee surveys and focus groups
2. A committee is established within the strategy team to analyze the engagement results and propose corrective actions
3. The strategy team uses the experience of reviewing engagement to plan a follow-up review in one year
4. Executives keep an eye on engagement but understand that it's not as important as other key metrics
5. The "engagement temperature" taken at this review is predicted to be the same the following year

Answer

Option 1: This option is correct. Surveys and focus groups are examples of both quantitative and qualitative methods you can use to assess engagement levels.

Option 2: This option is correct. When reviewing employee engagement levels, it's critical that action is taken after feedback is given.

Option 3: This option is correct. Engagement levels are only effective when they are continuously aligned with strategic objectives and monitored regularly.

Option 4: This option is incorrect. For strategic objectives to be implemented effectively, engagement metrics are critical as they need to be aligned with the organization's goals.

Option 5: This option is incorrect. Engagement levels can change at different times and for different reasons, so they need to be assessed each year.

Learning aid - Methods for Monitoring Strategy Execution

Monitoring method	What it involves
Action plans	Translate strategy maps into action plans for each employee
	Action steps include clearly-defined work assignments
	Individual names need to be assigned to each work assignment
	Draw up an organizational action plan listing each intended action step and work assignment in chronological order
	Decide when and where resources will need to be assigned for each department
Strategic dashboards	Establish electronic dashboards to view information from scorecards as well as detailed reports, statistical data, analyses, or graphs
	Enable those who use the dashboard to view the data in different formats, share information, and print various reports
	Enable those who view the dashboard to combine multiple views into a single display – this allows people to quickly assess the "health" of the organization at any given time
Strategic review meetings	All attendees must come to strategy review meetings fully prepared and aware of relevant issues and problems
	Discuss the progress of the organizational strategy map by tracking the scorecards of each department
	Encourage attendees to propose ways to improve performance and achieve goals
	The meetings shouldn't be used to alter strategy, but to solve any progress problems that have emerged from the data
Reviewing employee engagement	This method should be used to complement other monitoring methods
	Executives should take an "engagement temperature" at least once a year to monitor any changes. The method used to assess engagement should suit your particular organization and its operations
	Use surveys, interviews, and focus groups tailored to the organizational strategy to measure engagement.
	It's critical that you take corrective action on the results to rectify any drops in engagement
	To be effective these reviews should be conducted annually

Analyzing variance
Having a strategy that's appropriate and adaptable is critical for success. However, a strategy is useless if it can't be evaluated against results. Evaluating strategy provides information on strategy success and tests the logic that the organization's strategic objectives were built upon, making adjustments possible. By evaluating strategy, executives can also determine which employees should be rewarded for their work.

An important component of project evaluation is variance analysis. This involves assessing the differences between the intended objectives and the results achieved. Analyzing variance helps management to ascertain whether action is needed and, if so, what type of action is needed.

Many large strategic projects will generate numerous variances on a daily basis. To keep from being overwhelmed, businesses tend to focus on large variances only and ignore insignificant data, unless a trend emerges.

For example, a company analyzed the financial variances between the expected cost of using a subcontractor service and the actual cost. The difference was shown to be $1,000 but on only one occasion.

It's therefore ignored as a one-off, insignificant variance. A variance can't be ignored if it becomes a trend. If a trend had emerged – for instance, if invoices were consistently $1,000 or more over the expected price – it would become significant.

If this continued to rise over time, it would become a very significant variance for the company and the Purchasing Department would require investigation of its competence. Management would need to take action and investigate why it continues to differ from expected costs.

As an organization becomes more adept at analyzing variance and trends in variance, it learns to decide which fluctuations in the data to concentrate on. As the progress of a project is monitored and evaluated, management must decide which variances to respond to immediately, when to wait for a trend, or when to ignore variance.

Question

Which description correctly defines variance when evaluating strategy success?

Options:

1. Variance is the difference between the results produced and the outcome that was originally intended

2. Variance is a term used to describe an increasing trend in supplier costs

3. Variance is when management decides to take varying actions in response to project results

Answer

Business Execution

Option 1: This is the correct option. In general, variance is any difference between the objectives of a strategy and the actual results produced.

Option 2: This option is incorrect. Analyzing variance involves assessing the difference between a project's expected outcomes and the actual outcomes.

Option 3: This option is incorrect. Variance is the difference between expected and actual outcomes. It may lead to action being taken, or the variance may be ignored.

Management reports and actions

Evaluation usually takes place once the implementation process is underway and it's continuous throughout the execution of a strategy. The strategic planning process itself should also be reviewed. As successes and failures of a particular strategy are highlighted, the organization learns more each time about which planning processes are working best. During evaluation, the organization should aim to produce only a modest amount of information. It can be difficult interpreting information if there's too much or too little of it.

Evaluating a strategy and proposing adjustments usually involves changes to vision, the strategy map, achievement targets, or the program.

Formal strategy maps can be difficult to change once implementation is underway. If problems are identified within high-level strategic objectives, this may cause trouble throughout the organization, as objectives are cascaded down to individual actions. But strategy should not be seen as unchangeable.

There are four steps to evaluating organizational strategy. First, analyze management reports and identify actions that need to be taken. Second, assess and discuss priorities – which actions need to be taken first. Third, management needs to plan which corrective actions need to be implemented and approve them. Finally, the organization should also record and apply the lessons it has learned from the evaluation process.

The first step involves analyzing management reports in detail to assess variance in the data and to determine what the data points to in terms of successes and failures.

Management reports contain summaries from each department about how they have performed during the previous period. Key performance indicators, or KPIs, are included in the reports and point to successes and failures, such as sales increases, productivity rates, or customer retention numbers.

Management needs to ask if a strategy is working, as reflected in the KPIs, and if it isn't working, it needs to ask why. Then it can determine which variances should be given the highest priority.

Possible actions that result from analysis include correcting a simple flaw, investigating a variance's root cause, ignoring insignificant variances, and continuing to monitor to detect long-term trends. Actions and time lines are then assigned to the appropriate employees.

Consider this example. Executives at an energy company are analyzing management reports. The company's key strategy is to diversify into new energy products.

One of the objectives for this strategy was to increase the capability of the Research Department in terms of product development. Training and recruitment initiatives were introduced to create a highly-skilled Research Department. An associated KPI is an increase in expertise of the Research Department. This KPI was measured in an employee exam following an intensive training program on product development.

The management report shows that this KPI was not met as expected. There is a difference between the average score expected in the exam – over 80% – and the actual scores. Executives discuss what actions to take. They decide on a second round of training for the research employees to increase their skill level.

Question

Management at an online electronics store has a strategy of improving services to customers. It's currently evaluating this strategy by reviewing reports on its dashboard.

What steps should management take?

Options:

1. Management reports are analyzed in detail to detect variances between intended and actual outcomes of the strategy to improve customer service

2. A KPI to decrease the percentage of returns by 3% has not been met, so management agrees to monitor the variance for another two months

3. The head of the Customer Service Department is charged with monitoring the variance and must report back to management in two months

4. A KPI to decrease the percentage of returns has not been met, so management decides to revise the overall strategy

5. Management reworks the strategy map, as objectives are cascaded down to individual actions

Answer

Option 1: This option is correct. Results of metrics in the reports point to areas where the plan is veering away from its intended outcomes.

Option 2: This option is correct. Management evaluation of strategy often involves continuing to monitor a variance and seeing if trends emerge in the data.

Option 3: This option is correct. To ensure that the actions are carried out, relevant departments are assigned responsibility and time lines for their completion.

Option 4: This option is incorrect. Variances don't lead to abandonment of strategy but to corrective actions that are needed to get the strategy back on track.

Option 5: This option is incorrect. Sometimes evaluation can lead to changes in the overall strategy, but in this case, it's not necessary.

Assess and discuss priorities

The second step in the evaluation process is to assess priorities for dealing with these variances. You first need to establish which part of the strategy is causing the variances. Root causes of variance can include vision, the strategy map, achievement targets, or the program. Managers responsible for the part of the strategy that's causing the variance identify the root cause, assess its impact, and determine the required action.

In modern business operations there are often complex interplays between human resources and technology or other resources. It can be difficult to determine if the variance was caused by behavior or processes, or both. Therefore, there should be systems in place that highlight a variance as soon as it occurs.

When establishing the root cause of a variance, evaluators should look back at the strategy's initial intentions. What were the current circumstances and challenges that led to an objective being created? What strengths, weaknesses, internal capabilities, and external opportunities shaped the issue?

Once the organization has linked the variances to their causes, they can be prioritized based on their magnitude, the certainty of the trend, and their impact. The organization then needs to decide what actions need to be taken, and it needs to categorize each action item.

For example, a company might establish a three-part categorization system. The first category consists of issues that don't require immediate action but are recorded for continuous monitoring. The second consists of issues that may require action in the near future but become part of the organization's regular strategic planning process.

The third category might be for issues that require immediate action outside of the regular planning process. These issues are important as they may threaten the success of the organization in a significant way.

In their analysis of management reports, executives at the energy company uncovered a significant variance between expected and actual test scores. They also uncovered a small variance in the financial data, between expected and actual cost of recruiting research experts.

The team discussed the two variances and prioritized them. Because the variance between expected and actual cost of recruitment was under $2,000, the executives decided to ignore it as a once-off event.

The team decided that the test scores variance would require immediate action because if employees' level of expertise doesn't increase, the company's future success could be threatened.

Question

Management at an online electronics company is assessing and discussing priorities around evaluating the company's customer service strategy.

Which examples describe the elements involved in the second phase of evaluating strategy?

Options:

1. The root causes of the customer service strategy variances are investigated

2. Executives develop a system for categorizing issues and prioritize the need to achieve a decrease in percentage of returns

3. Management reviews the high number of returns and customer dissatisfaction issues that framed the strategy

4. Management creates a plan to immediately deal with each variance it discovers 5. Management picks the variances that are easiest to fix and prioritizes them

Answer

Option 1: This option is correct. Management should try to establish which element of the strategy a variance relates to.

Option 2: This option is correct. Categorizing which issues need to be acted upon more urgently helps the organization to prioritize and adapt.

Option 3: This option is correct. Each issue in the strategy is framed by elements that affect the organization. Knowing these helps to come up with solutions to variances.

Option 4: This option is incorrect. Variances should be discussed and prioritized. Some are dealt with immediately, some are monitored, and some are ignored.

Business Execution

Option 5: This option is incorrect. Priorities should be established based on their magnitude and the impact on the organization.

Plan corrective actions

The third step in the process is planning what corrective actions to take to address areas that may be associated with the root cause of a variance – the organization's vision, strategy map, achievement targets, or the program itself.

See each of the areas that may be associated with the root cause of a variance to learn more about it.

Vision

If the root cause of the variance lies in the organization's vision, you may need to revise it. This should be handled carefully as it will affect the entire company and possibly involve actions in other change categories.

Strategy map

A root cause identified in the strategy map is common.

For example, expected sales didn't materialize because the sales objectives were rendered redundant by changes in the market. This would make the strategy map's overall objective irrelevant.

Achievement targets

Identifying that changes are required to reach achievement targets is very common. Targets are often adjusted so that they're once again relevant to the strategy.

For example, initial targets may have been unrealistic – set too high – or have proven to be impossible to measure.

Program

Changes to the strategic program itself are often required. In some cases, the entire program has to be adjusted.

However, implementing change to the program can be quite complex, as changes to the program cascade down to the various components of the program. Having a formal process for program changes helps to prevent changes from being made when they aren't necessary.

As management plans corrective actions within one or more of the key change categories, it considers a number of options. Correcting a root cause of variance might involve altering an organization's structure, replacing one or more key individuals, selling a division, or revising a business mission, for example. They may be large- or small-scale changes.

Consider the energy company as it carries out the third step of evaluation. Executives plan corrective actions for the test score variance. They identify the root cause of the variance as being part of the program itself.

They agree that the training program needs to be slightly adjusted to ensure that the scores can be improved. Fortunately, adapting this part of the program won't disrupt the rest of the strategy too much as the problem has been isolated within the planning of the training initiative.

Question

Management at an online electronics company is now planning corrective actions for variances discovered.

Which statements describe what might be involved in this third stage of strategy evaluation?

Options:

1. Management reviews change categories of vision, strategy map, achievement targets, and the program to make changes

2. Management makes changes to the program carefully as they may affect other components of the strategy

3. Management decides that the achievement targets are also unrealistic and unmeasurable 4. Management adopts the same corrective actions as another organization

5. Management decides to allow changes to be made to the program as often as possible

Answer

Option 1: This option is correct. The root cause of variance is identified in one or more of these categories and then corrective actions are agreed upon.

Option 2: This option is correct. Components of a strategy are often interconnected and cascaded through the organization, so changes need to be considered carefully.

Option 3: This option is correct. A strategy may be fine but the achievement targets may need to be corrected to make them relevant to current circumstances.

Option 4: This option is incorrect. Corrective actions might involve selling a business division or replacing individuals, for example, but they should suit the particular organization's situation.

Option 5: This option is incorrect. A program may require change but because it affects other categories, a formal change system should be in place.

Record and apply lessons

The fourth and final step in the evaluation process is to record lessons learned. Organizations should use this process as an opportunity to continually learn more about their own strategic planning processes. The lessons learned from successes and failures in planning should be documented and circulated to all involved.

Strategic planning, identifying issues and variances, and applying corrective actions are part of a continuous cycle for successful organizations. Evaluation involves continuous assessment and improvement, and lessons learned play a key role in this.

Circumstances will always change and organizations must be able to adapt their strategies to suit the new circumstances. Incorporating the lessons learned from repeated planning processes into the organization's policies helps it to continuously improve.

Consider how the energy company implemented the final step in evaluating execution. Once the training initiative was highlighted for adjustment, the team reviewed the lessons learned.

The team concluded that it should have worked harder to ensure the training initiative was comprehensive and detailed enough to deliver an 80% pass rate for the test. The team decided that, in the future, it would consider in much more detail how to implement the strategy so that it achieves the desired results.

The lessons learned were incorporated into the strategic planning document and circulated to all the teams involved.

Question

An online electronics company is carrying out the final phase of evaluation.

Which statements characterize how it might record and apply lessons?

Options:

1. Management allocates resources to the corrective action of changing the program

2. Management records what it has learned about the strategic review process and distributes it to the relevant people

3. Management decides to continue using the planning processes it has used in the past, regardless of new variances uncovered

4. Only a few key executives are involved in learning lessons from the strategic planning process

Answer

Option 1: This option is correct. Once corrective actions have been approved, management must agree on what resources need to be allocated to complete them.

Option 2: This option is correct. Successes and failures uncovered in variances help to indicate changes needed in the overall planning process.

Option 3: This option is incorrect. Organizations should use variances to learn lessons about their planning processes and incorporate them into planning policies.

Option 4: This option is incorrect. The lessons learned should be incorporated into planning policy and circulated to all involved.

Case Study: Question 1 of 2
Scenario

The executives of a marketing company have analyzed management reports as part of a strategic evaluation. One of the company's key objectives was to increase turnover within the Internet advertising sector. The executives used metrics on sales figures and customer numbers to assess this objective. A variance was uncovered between expected customer acquisition numbers and actual acquisition numbers. Because there has been a consistent variance over the last three quarters, the executives decide to prioritize this variance.

Answer the questions in order.

Question

The executives reviewed the organization's mission. They discovered that the achievement targets for the objective were inappropriate because they didn't accurately measure sales. Although customer numbers hadn't increased as expected, sales from existing customers had grown considerably. The executives then looked at other change categories that might be affecting the variance. Once they knew the reason for the variance, they were happy to carry on with the existing strategy as it was.

In what ways has the evaluation process been implemented correctly?

Options:

1. An undesirable trend was uncovered from analyzing management reports and this was prioritized

2. The root cause of the variance was identified as being within the strategy's achievement targets

3. The executives were right to take no corrective action to fix the variance

4. The executives learned that they had made an error in planning, but kept it to themselves

Answer

Option 1: This option is correct. Analyzing management reports and prioritizing actions are the first two steps of evaluating strategy.

Option 2: This option is correct. Establishing which change category is the root cause of the variance is part of the third step in evaluation – planning corrective action.

Option 3: This option is incorrect. Once the root cause was identified, the executives should have planned appropriate actions to correct it.

Option 4: This option is incorrect. The executives should have recorded and applied the lessons learned to continuously improve the planning process.

Case Study: Question 2 of 2

Scenario

The executives of a marketing company have analyzed management reports as part of a strategic evaluation. One of the company's key objectives was to increase turnover within the Internet advertising sector. The executives used metrics on sales figures and customer numbers to assess this objective. A variance was uncovered between expected customer acquisition numbers and actual acquisition numbers. Because there has been a consistent variance over the last three quarters, the executives decide to prioritize this variance.

Answer the questions in order.

Question

The team then looked at other change categories that might be affecting the variance.

How could the executive team have improved its evaluation process?

Options:

1. Once they identified the root cause of the variance, the executives should have adjusted the strategy map by removing customer numbers as an achievement target

2. The team should have changed the planning policy so that more appropriate achievement targets are selected in the future

3. The executives shouldn't have prioritized the variance they uncovered because it wasn't significant

4. The team shouldn't have looked at other change categories in addition to achievement targets when identifying the root cause

Answer

Option 1: This option is correct. Sales are higher than ever, so customer numbers became an inappropriate achievement target for the strategy.

Option 2: This option is correct. Learning and applying lessons to the planning process is an important part of strategy evaluation.

Option 3: This option is incorrect. The variance was consistent over three quarters, so it became a trend that was having an impact on the strategy.

Option 4: This option is incorrect. This variance in achievement targets will also require a change to the wording of the objectives in the strategy map as increasing customer numbers is no longer a key objective.

Learning aid - Guide to Evaluating Strategy Execution

Steps in evaluation	What it involves
Analyze management reports and identify actions	Identify variances from management reports and results of metrics
	Establish root causes by investigating which part of the strategy variations are associated with
	Assess the impact of each variance and determine whether to address the variance or ignore it
Assess and discuss priorities	Categorize each variance by whether it should be monitored more, included in the regular strategy planning meeting, or acted upon immediately
Plan corrective actions	Decide which corrective actions to take by making changes to the organization's vision, strategy map, achievement targets, or the program itself
	Identify how the actions can be facilitated – what resources need to be allocated, who should be assigned responsibility, and how long it should take to complete the task
Record and apply lessons	Have the successes and failures of the strategy led to any lessons learned about the planning process in general? If so, record these lessons and circulate them to all involved
	Incorporate lessons learned into strategy planning policy

Activity - **Reflecting on Evaluation of Execution**

To use this tool, print the document and write your answers to the questions in the table provided. Alternatively, use a word processing or spreadsheet application to create a simple table using the same questions.

1. What difficulties did I encounter in isolating issues and causes?
2. How did I decide which issues to prioritize?
3. What was the outcome of the evaluation in terms of corrective actions?
4. Did I learn any lessons from the evaluation and how did I implement what I learned?
5. What would have helped the process be more successful?

Why strategy ceases to work
   Strategy comes full circle after it has been evaluated. The organization's vision, strategy map, achievement targets, and a program of execution are all analyzed during strategy development. Once evaluation of execution has taken place, these components of strategy then become areas of change. The root causes of variances discovered during evaluation are linked back to one or more of these change categories. Corrective action is then taken to realign strategy to the organization's current needs.
   There are a number of key benefits to revising strategy. Reassessment of strategy helps organizations to remain responsive to important issues. It also ensures that strategies remain effective. The lessons learned from revision help the organization improve its knowledge and internal collaboration. Finally uncovering what works and what needs improvement fosters energy and motivation for change.

See each benefit of strategy to learn more about it.

Remain responsive

Organizations can become stuck in certain response patterns, reacting to old problems that are no longer an issue. Regular reassessment and revision of strategy is necessary to ensure that the organization is responding to real problems and customer demand.

Strategies remain effective

Even if strategies are responding to real problems and issues, it's important to ensure they are still effective in doing this over a long period of time. A strategy may be appropriate to the organization's objectives but may encounter smaller implementation issues along the way that need to be addressed.

Improve knowledge and collaboration

As information about strategic progress is cascaded down through the organization, knowledge is increased. Each department 'is aware of what's currently needed to execute strategic objectives. Interaction and collaboration between various departments is improved as awareness increases. As strategies are revised, decision making throughout the company becomes geared toward the common goal.

Foster energy and motivation

Minor problems are usually addressed through regular administrative channels, but strategy reassessment inspires ideas, energy, and motivation for improvement. Circumstances change and reassessing the strategy becomes a time for creativity and thinking "outside the box." This completes the loop as fresh ideas and objectives lead to a new round in strategic planning.

External circumstances and internal priorities will always change over time. Strategies need continuous monitoring to ensure that they remain effective and address the current challenges.

Even for strategies that are working well, continuous evaluation of implementation will lead to reassessment and revision to ensure that they continue to remain effective.

And strategies that are shown to be ineffective should be replaced by more appropriate plans of action.

So why do strategies cease to work? A strategy can fail for a number of reasons. First, a strategy may be appropriate but have insufficient resources devoted to it and therefore it cannot be executed correctly. Second, the environment may change, affecting the relevance of a strategy as people's attention shifts to other areas. Third, the initial issue or problem that the strategy is based on may have changed. And fourth, there may have been too many strategic objectives applied.

See each of the four main reasons for strategy failure to learn more about it.

Insufficient resources

If a strategic objective isn't assigned enough resources, its chances of success are significantly reduced.

For example, a company might decide to introduce a successful new product in one year. However, if the Research and Development Department isn't provided with sufficient financial and human resources to develop the product, it's unlikely that it will come up with a successful product.

Environment changes

The political environment within an organization may lead to the strategy losing momentum or being ignored completely.

For example, an executive at a company drives and champions a new quality control initiative. When the executive retires, he is replaced by an executive who is convinced that quality is not an issue – the caliber of employees is. So the initiative is stalled half way to completion and all attention is shifted away from it.

Issue or problem has changed

The issues and problems that a strategy was initially designed to address may change, making the current strategy no longer relevant. The implementation of a good strategy may cause complications, so what was once a good plan for addressing a problem could become a problem itself. This situation prompts the need for a new strategy map.

For example, an international clothing label has a strategy of expanding its brick and mortar outlets to access its young customers worldwide. Research shows that the company's customers are increasingly buying over the Internet, so the strategy becomes obsolete.

Too many objectives

Strategies may be all-encompassing and complex, but their overarching objectives should be focused and clear. If a strategy has too many objectives, particularly ones that are competing with one another, it may collapse under the strain.

For example, a company might have three objectives that involve expansion and new services and two objectives that involve cost cutting. These objectives may conflict with one another as one involves investment and the other involves saving. The many smaller objectives cascaded down through the organization may make the entire strategy overly complex and unworkable.

Question

Which statements demonstrate examples of what might cause a strategy to fail?

Options:

1. A new manager who doesn't agree with the existing innovation strategy works toward her preferred goals instead

2. A strategy was established to steal market share from a competitor that is no longer in business

3. A company implements a strategy of international expansion but doesn't have the resources to investigate suitable markets

4. An organization adopts a complex financial strategy that includes several contradictory objectives

5. A company adopts a customer-focused strategy with multiple strategic objectives that affect all departments

6. A company's expansion strategy fails to deliver results because the strategy has been in place for a long time

Answer

Option 1: This option is correct. Environment changes, such as the recruitment of new managers, may result in the strategy being ignored.

Option 2: This option is correct. One of the reasons strategy ceases to work is that the initial issue that prompted it has changed.

Option 3: This option is correct. Insufficient resources devoted to implementation can cause a good objective to fail.

Option 4: This option is correct. Having too many objectives can sometimes lead to a strategy being misaligned and impossible to implement.

Option 5: This option is incorrect. A strategy with many objectives can still work if the interconnections between objectives are clear and aligned.

Option 6: This option is incorrect. Long-term strategies can work if monitored and implemented correctly.

The time to change

Once problems are identified and their root cause investigated, those accountable need to follow through on fixing them. If the results aren't as expected, either the strategy or the tactics you use to implement it need to change. A strategy may be sound, but you may be using the wrong tactics to implement it. Alternatively, your tactics may make sense, but what you're trying to achieve may not be relevant.

It's important to remember that while reassessment and revision of strategic plans is necessary, changes may not always be needed. This is particularly true for long-term strategic goals.

If the evaluation indicates that there are no major changes in the external environment or within the organization's capabilities to proceed with the plan, the strategy should be allowed to proceed.

Organizations should observe whether plans are proceeding on schedule and whether goals and objectives are being realized as predicted. If the anticipated results are being achieved, then the existing strategy is working.

If the plans aren't delivering the goals and objectives intended, the strategy will need to be revised.

Some managers are reluctant to revisit the strategy. Such individuals see the strategy as a concrete plan that shouldn't be messed with. Perhaps it took a long time to devise in the first place, and they feel it should remain, no matter what the circumstances.

Reluctance to revisit and revise the strategy in the face of changing circumstances will lead to failure. As things change, managers need to call the team together and ask "How does this affect our strategy?" and "What do we need to do to our strategy to incorporate this change?".

Reflect

Think about a time that a change threatened a current strategy in your organization. How did you deal with this?

Write down your response or enter it in a text file in your word-processor application (or in a text editor such as Notepad) and save it to your hard drive for later viewing.

Your response may have included consulting with your team as a first step in altering your strategy. As changing circumstances emerge, you should consult key decision makers, implementers, and beneficiaries about how to deal with the new threats or opportunities.

In doing this, you will need to broaden your circle of collaborators beyond the team who devised the existing strategy. Leaders will need the support of a different team to get new ideas and action plans.

Consulting a new team on how to alter the strategy helps to get buy-in for the new plan that is to be implemented.

Steps to altering strategy

When altering strategy, there are four steps to help focus on the problem and its solution. The first is to focus on the mission of the organization and its strategic direction. Second, try to coordinate the systems and execution processes already in place. In the third step, discuss ways to realign the culture of the organization to empower people for strategy execution. And fourth, communicate the revisions and changes that have been made to ensure that lessons are learned.

Consider the example of a large information storage services company. It has become clear to executives that the current objective of increasing product range within the information storage market isn't working. As part of the first step in altering the strategy, a team meets to focus on the organization's mission and strategic direction.

The team comes to the conclusion that the current strategy has lost sight of the company's original strategic mission, which was to continuously provide the most up-to-date data storage solutions to large companies. The current strategy is focused on filing cabinets, archive boxes, and other related physical solutions to store information.

The market has changed and large companies are now turning to electronic forms of data management such as cloud services. This has become a much more cost-effective way of storing and managing large volumes of information for their clients.

Question

How did the team in the previous example implement the first step of altering strategy – focus on mission and direction?

Options:

1. The team decided that the current strategy lost sight of the company's original strategic aim, which was to continuously provide up-to-date storage solutions

2. The team discussed how the results of metrics involving customer numbers support the existing strategy

3. The team discussed how the strategy of providing filing systems had been wrong all along

Answer

Option 1: This is the correct option. The team realized that the current strategy is no longer addressing the mission to provide the most efficient data management services to customers.

Option 2: This option is incorrect. To alter strategy, the first step is to return to basics and focus on mission and direction.

Option 3: This option is incorrect. The strategy aligned with the mission in the past but now needs to be altered to match new circumstances.

When the team meets to discuss altering a strategy, the second step is to discuss how to coordinate systems. An organization might have good strategic objectives, plus the commitment of various departments, but if departments aren't tightly integrated, it makes it harder for strategy to succeed.

Going back to the data storage example, the team now knows that it needs to invest resources into developing a more IT-driven solution to data storage. This opens the company up to a whole new market and a new set of competitors in the form of IT firms. The company will need to harness the expertise that already exists in its IT and Marketing Departments to implement the new product strategy.

To ensure successful execution, these departments, along with the Finance Department, will need to adopt systems for working closely together across different geographical locations. One of the things they decide to do is to invest in web conferencing software to enable more integrated product development and strategy execution.

A key part of ensuring buy-in for the altered strategy is realigning the culture with the new plan. Often employees understand and are inspired by an organization's vision, but they need to be empowered to ensure it's executed effectively. These employees understand the problems they're facing and that the values of the organization have been successfully instilled. However, if the culture isn't aligned and employees aren't empowered, they can't help transform the organization.

Blocks to decision making must be removed if employees are to adopt new behaviors that support the vision and strategy.

In fast-moving environments, the process of strategic reviews being cascaded in a top-down fashion can be too slow when it comes to adapting to problems on the ground. Employees on the front line need to understand the vision and strategic objectives and be empowered to make decisions based on this when a fast response is vital.

In the data storage example, the staff in the company's retail stores has only been trained in selling the older solutions for data storage. To realign the culture with the strategy alterations, employees will need to be trained in selling the merits of cloud services. The IT executives who are developing the new services also need to be empowered to make key decisions. They do this based on their expertise and their understanding of the company's vision and mission.

Question

In the previous example, what did the team do to coordinate systems and processes, realign culture, and empower employees?

Options:

1. The team coordinated its internal systems so that departments could work together from different locations

2. The team discussed the organizational culture and then looked at how each retail store cooperates with one another

3. The team reviewed the mission of the company and then decided to change the culture and provide new services

4. The team trained employees in selling the merits of cloud services and empowered executives to make decisions

Answer

Option 1: This option is correct. The second step – coordinating systems – and the third step – realigning strategy – both help to keep execution on track.

Option 2: This option is incorrect. The second step of altering strategy involves coordinating systems and the third involves realigning strategy.

Option 3: This option is incorrect. After reviewing the mission, the second step is to coordinate systems and the third is to realign culture with the strategy.

Option 4: This option is correct. Empowering employees and realigning the culture to the strategy are key steps in altering strategy.

The final step in ensuring successful strategy alteration is to communicate revisions and changes throughout the organization. Communication can be through informal meetings, large scale conferences, or newsletters, for example. Employees should regularly be made aware of the connection between their efforts and the results being achieved. The new vision and strategic objectives should be inspiring and encourage buy-in from as many employees as possible. Once employees understand the need for change and see results, the new strategy becomes instilled.

The team in the data storage example develops the new cloud data management services and markets it to new and existing clients.

Throughout the development process, employees were informed through meetings and newsletters of the need for this change. Input was encouraged from employees who had ideas about how to ensure the new strategy succeeds.

By the time the new service is being marketed and sold, employees are completely on board with the new strategy and understand how it aligns with the organizational mission. Regular communication has ensured that staff is motivated and empowered to sell the new service in the best way possible. This gives the new strategy its best chance of success.

Question

A manufacturing company evaluates its strategy and discovers that its current strategy needs to be revised. One of its key objectives was to deliver orders faster than its competitors. However, it's now emerging that this strategy isn't paying off, as many orders have been defective.

Which statements represent examples of what the company should do to revise the strategy?

Options:

1. The company should form a team to focus on the mission of providing the best products possible

2. The company should coordinate its systems so that the production line is focused on the objective of quality

3. Quality control employees should be empowered to make decisions on the spot to reduce the number of defective goods

4. The company should ensure that it communicates the need for change to all employees

5. The company should continue with the current strategy and sell the defective goods at a lower price

6. The company should only give authority to high-level executives to oversee quality control

Answer

Option 1: This option is correct. The current strategy of fast delivery has lost sight of the company's mission – to provide the best quality products.

Option 2: This option is correct. Coordinating systems is the second step of altering strategy and helps ensure better execution.

Option 3: This option is correct. The third step of altering strategy involves realigning culture and empowering employees.

Option 4: This option is correct. Communicating vision and strategy helps to ensure that change is institutionalized.

Option 5: This option is incorrect. The defective goods are a result of rushing orders and this doesn't align with the company's mission of offering high-quality goods.

Option 6: This option is incorrect. The best way to ensure successful execution is to empower frontline employees to make decisions quickly.

CHAPTER FIVE
Resources & Glossary

Glossary

B

balanced scorecard - Also known as BSC, a strategic planning and management system used to align business activities to the mission, values, or vision statements of an organization.

BSC - See balanced scorecard.

business culture - Also known as culture, this is the shared beliefs, attitudes, and behaviors of employees in an organization.

business execution - The process of implementing a plan or strategy with the aim of achieving a specific business goal.

C

cascading BSC - Linking business unit or department scorecards to the highest level corporate scorecard. All business unit or department scorecards combined should cover all of the high level objectives. See also balanced scorecard.

competency - The level of knowledge or skills required by an individual to perform a job properly.

culture - See business culture.

I

individual development plan - A plan tailored for specific employees that identifies areas of skill, knowledge, or abilities that the employee must develop in order to support an organization's goals.

M

mission statement - A brief statement that defines the purpose of the organization, including what it will provide to its customers.

N

norms - Socially shared standards that lead individuals to conform.

S

strategic initiative - Short-term action that launches an organization on a trajectory toward achieving its vision.

strategy - Corporate decisions about what the business should do and how resources should be allocated. These decisions take into account competitive conditions and growth opportunities.

strategy direction statement - A statement differentiating a company's position and product offering from competitors.

V

values statement - A statement that reflects the attitude, behavior and character of an organization.

vision statement - A statement that defines the long term goals of an organization.

Resources
1. *The Workforce Scorecard—Managing Human Capital to Execute Strategy* - 2005, Mark A. Huselid, Brian E. Becker, and Richard W. Beatty, Harvard Business Press
2. *Making Strategy Work: Leading Effective Execution and Change (A Summary)* - 2005, Lawrence G. Hrebiniak, Soundview Executive Book Summaries
3. *The Execution Premium: Linking Strategy to Operations for Competitive Advantage* - 2008, Robert S. Kaplan and David P. Norton, Harvard Business Press
4. *Making Strategy Work—The Complete Summary Making Strategy Work: Leading Effective Execution and Change (A Summary)* - 2005, Lawrence G. Hrebiniak , Soundview Executive Book Summaries

5. *The Execution Premium: Linking Strategy to Operations for Competitive Advantage* - 2008, Robert S. Kaplan and David P. Norton, Harvard Business Press
6. *Execution: The Discipline of Getting Things Done* - 2002, Larry Bossidy and Ram Charan, Soundview Executive Book Summaries
7. *Strategic Management: From Theory to Implementation, Fourth Edition* - 1998, David Hussey, Butterworth-Heinemann
8. *Making Strategy Work: Leading Effective Execution and Change* - 2005, Lawrence G. Hrebiniak, Soundview Executive Book Summaries
9. *Strategic DNA: Bringing Business Strategy to Life* - 2008, Lawrence Hobbs
10. *Strategic Planning for Public and Nonprofit Organizations: A Guide to Strengthening and Sustaining Organizational Achievement* - 2004, John M. Bryson, Jossey-Bass

www.ingramcontent.com/pod-product-compliance
Lightning Source LLC
Chambersburg PA
CBHW020900180526
45163CB00007B/2570